# ANIMAL SOUL

# ANIMAL SOUL

JOHN C. WOODCOCK

iUniverse, Inc.
Bloomington

# Animal Soul

*iUniverse books may be ordered through booksellers or by contacting:*

*iUniverse*
*1663 Liberty Drive*
*Bloomington, IN 47403*
*www.iuniverse.com*
*1-800-Authors (1-800-288-4677)*

*ISBN: 978-1-4759-5064-9 (sc)*
*ISBN: 978-1-4759-5065-6 (ebk)*

*Printed in the United States of America*

*iUniverse rev. date: 09/25/2012*

*The way I conceive it, our being-in-the-world itself IS soul. "Soul" is nothing particular, but rather the name for the very nature of human being-in-the-world itself. Therefore there is no exit out of soul, or of soul out of the world (other than the literal end of our being-in-the-world). There is only the possibility of transformations, metamorphoses, reconstitutions of "soul", from an archaic mythic via . . . . to a modern form and definition of soul. No alternative. Inescapable. Soul is always. Soul is (a) the presupposition of the field of psychology and (b) the factually existing presupposition as which human existence is.*

Wolfgang Giegerich (online discussion-permission granted)

# CONTENTS

# PREFACE

This is a book of analysis and auguries. As an "analyst", I acknowledge my several teachers who taught me how to *think*, to wield and endure the "cut" of the animus into the innocent allurement of the image. As an augur, I follow the way of "quiet whispers . . . of the signs . . . all those irrational moments when one feels the portent of the uncertain and unknown future." [1]

All my adult life I have moved between that pair of opposites: the *Pontifices* and the *Augures*, which I suspect may be a true dialectical opposition. At times I have spoken *ex cathedra* (pontificating) and at others I have sounded ponderously *mysterious*, as one early teacher suggested.

I believe this pair is working through me as a dialectical opposition because, in spite of my greatest efforts, I have been unable to write exclusively in the one "voice" or the other. For example I may be writing an analytical piece and a dream will "pop up" in the middle of it, which I do not ignore. The thesis of my doctorate was written this way occasioning an interesting "invention" of a methodology to justify it. As I wrote in a "Back Cover" to one of my other books, this form of literature seems to involve:

*. . . spontaneous weaving of realities that we normally keep well apart. This writing moves from a memory to a dream to a reflection of an external event, to an etymological study of a word, to the words of another author until the usual separation of inner and outer dissolves . . .*

---

[1]  (Lockhart, 1987, p. 48)

If this is a living dialectic at work in my life then presumably there is a "unity of the unity and difference" implict in these opposites I have "suffered" for so long. Until this unity is made explicit to me, no doubt books such as the one just written will strike the reader in terms of the movements between the two modes. I can only hope an underlying unity can be discerned as well.

# INTRODUCTION

## OUR MODE OF EXISTENCE TODAY

Figure 1

*When you have to solve such an important problem that is really new to the age, you will be tremendously influenced by the way in which this problem has been answered hitherto . . . and the solution proposed by old Zarathustra was: Let the spirit overcome matter . . . the existence of matter will be wiped out. [This] appears in Christianity, where hell-fire comes at the end of our days and the whole world is burnt up. [It] appears in the primitive Germanic religions, where in the end the ferocious wolf will appear and the world will be devoured by fire . . . which accounts for all the conclusions drawn by Christianity concerning the neglect or destruction of the body . . . everything which was concerned with the body was low or vulgar.*

C. G. Jung

*Those instincts of wild, free, prowling man became turned backwards against man himself. Enmity, cruelty the delight in persecution, in surprises, change, destruction—the turning all these instincts against their own possessors: this is the origin of the "bad conscience". It was man, who, lacking external enemies and obstacles, and imprisoned as he was in the oppressive narrowness and monotony of custom, in his own impatience lacerated, persecuted, gnawed, frightened, and ill-treated himself; it was this animal in the hands of the tamer which beat itself against the bars of its cage; it was this being who, pining and yearning for that desert home of which it had been deprived, was compelled to create out of its own self, an adventure, a torture chamber, a hazardous and perilous desert—it was this fool this homesick and desperate prisoner—who invented the "bad conscience." But thereby he introduced that most grave and sinister illness, from which mankind has not yet recovered, the suffering of man from the disease called man, as the result of a violent breaking from his animal past, the result, as it were, of a spasmodic plunge into a new environment and new conditions of existence, the result of a declaration of war against the old instincts which up to that time had been the staple of his power, his joy, his formidableness.*

Nietzsche

The two quotes above, one by C. G. Jung and one by Nietzsche, address the development of Western civilization as founded on the principle of spirit overcoming matter or spirit overcoming the natural animal wisdom that once guided and informed our earthly existence. This process of overcoming the "natural things", is now reaching its nadir as the now ruling principle of the economy with its mincing machine of the advertising industry establishes its total dominance of our lives. The advertising industry has succeeded in reducing all things in the "natural world" to an abstract content that has no meaning. For example, what was once a living animal with its wisdom, mystery and mentoring of human affairs has become a label for a shoe, or a logo for a company. All meaning that was once intrinsic to the animal is lost. An animal is merely a *product* like everything else.

There are many serious attempts to *restore* our connection to the divinity of animals or more broadly the sacredness of nature, emerging from within the ecology or environmental movements by appeal to the psychology of C. G. Jung and his notion of the archetypes. Since we no longer experience the divinity of animals or nature outwardly, Jung "discovered" that we can find our way to that experience inwardly or through the unconscious where dream animals may "speak" to us, guide or terrify us as they once did outwardly. We may even have an archetypal experience of the animal "within". This is felt by some theorists to be the way to a restoration of what seems to be an outwardly irrevocable loss. The argument is that if we can recover that connection inwardly through numinous experiences then we will be opened up to the sacred dimension of nature and animals outwardly once more. In this way we can, the argument goes, somehow restore a balance to our dealings with nature, and oppose or counter the seemingly unstoppable rape of nature taking place today: [2]

*The basic premise of ecopsychology is that we have a deep-seated layer of our psyche in which we remain "at one" with the world. This layer has been covered over by civilization, education, and modernity, but it is rescuable from the dark dungeons of the past, or from what Jung would call the deeper reaches of the unconscious. If we can take risks with our consciousness, we might be able to dive deep into the psyche and bring up these lost, forgotten, or overlaid layers of mind. Jung refers to this forgotten vestige as the "two-million—year-old man that is in all of us. He personifies it as an archetypal figure and urges the modern man or woman to get in touch with this figure in the psyche, and to draw from it the wisdom that has been lost in the modern period. "It is only possible to live the fullest life when we are in harmony with these symbols; wisdom is a return to them. (337)*

---

[2]   (Tacey, 2010)

I see no sign whatsoever that such a theoretical move is having any effect whatsoever in the real world. As I wrote elsewhere: [3]

*. . . the devastation continues at an alarming rate. We all know this and only have to turn on the TV for 5 minutes to see another instance paraded before our eyes, such as the recent news of the live export of cattle to Indonesia from Australia and the horrific treatment they receive before finally being slaughtered. With this example we can see that the arguments put forward either to stop live exports or resume them do not hold any mention, not even the merest whisper of cattle being "divine" and for that reason should be treated differently. No at best there is talk of "humane slaughter" rather than cruelty, but they will be slaughtered no matter what! The mighty engine of economics WILL have the last say, of that you can be sure.*

The effort of re-awakening our connection to the sacredness of animals and nature by *persuading* us through arguments based on the discovery of, for example, numinous animal images "in" the unconscious are doomed from the start. Our ancestors (probably as far back as the hunter-gather times) had no need for such persuasion. That nature was an expression of divinity was self-evident. Nature *spoke* to human beings, initiated them through her Master animals, and gave freely of her wisdom so that human beings could align themselves with life, even to the point of going to their own death with dignity.

The fact that a case has to be *argued* for the sacred nature of animals is an affirmation that we have irrevocably lost what our ancestors took for granted. We have no chance of any such immediate experience of nature. Our relationship to the world today is a highly reflected one, as Tarnas puts it: [4]

*The world does not exist as a thing-in-itself, independent of interpretation; rather it comes into being only in and through interpretations. The subject of knowledge is already embedded in the object of knowledge . . . human experience is linguistically,*

---

3    (Woodcock, 2011)

4    (Tarnas, 1991)

*prestructured, yet the various structures of language possess no demonstrable connection with independent reality.* (397)

The 20th century came to understand that we are inextricably enclosed in language and our experience of the world cannot be separated from our interpretations. This is a highly reflected state of being. To put it another way, the soul once reflected its realities in the natural things, and *presented* itself to human beings in an *immediate* sense. Nature and animal divinity was self-presentational, innocent, taken as "just so".

Today the soul has withdrawn from the natural things as medium for its self-expression, transformed and is reflecting itself in language and we modern people *can* only discern soul processes in and through language.[5]

This was a slow process at first as the *divinity* (a property of soul life) of nature slowly withdrew from nature and settled in human beings who came to feel themselves as conscious subjects, each with a free will and carrying an aspect of divinity. We have built our culture and civilization accordingly. Descartes as we know inaugurated the movement towards a complete separation between spirit (as subjectivity or *res cogitans*) and matter (*res extensa*) and our culture has not looked back since.

Today we have arrived at a very complex set of psychological conditions. We recognize *in theory* that we and the world do not exist independently, that the world or "nature" is "largely man himself reflected and by that reflection, disguised." At the same time *in actual experience* we each feel ourselves to be a "merely spatial centre, psychically as well as physically isolated from the outside world and from its fellow units".[6]

We have in fact become psychologically separate from our own bodies, our feelings, and even our thoughts. Separation from our bodies leaves our bodies of course as "things" that can be operated upon. The best linguistic expression of this separation lies within the rhetoric and practices of our modern medicine.

---

[5]   (Giegerich, 2010c, p. 218 ff)

[6]   (Barfield, 1977, p. 182)

The most compelling medium showing how far we have separated from our feelings is of course television and the movie industry both of which bring home the news that the most anguished emotional outpouring is in fact only a show, or entertainment (obviously I am distinguishing the logic of the media from the personal experience of the people who are thus "anguishing"). Separation from even our thoughts is disclosed in the syntax of the most vigorous political or other debates (talk shows etc.) where opinions are allowed (in the name of democracy) but almost never taken seriously, rarely leading to a change of mind in the other.

I found a compelling example from the media recently which revealed very clearly the degree of separation that obtains today, between consciousness and empirical life.

*How I Ended This Summer* from Russia was released in 2011—a movie which starkly demonstrates our modern mode of consciousness: [7]

Figure 2

---

[7]   (Film Movement, 2011)

*On a desolate island in the Arctic Circle, two men work at a small meteorological station, taking readings from their radioactive surroundings. Sergei, a gruff professional in his fifties, takes his job very seriously. His new partner, bright eyed college grad Pavel, retreats to his MP3 player and video games to avoid Sergei's imposing presence. One day while Sergei is out, inexperienced Pavel receives terrible news for Sergei from HQ. Intimidated, Pavel can't bring himself to disclose the information. When the truth is finally revealed, the consequences explode against a chilling backdrop of thick fog, sharp rocks, and the merciless Arctic Sea.*

This synopsis places the human beings at the centre, making the plot a human story set "against a chilling backdrop of thick fog, sharp rocks, and the merciless Arctic Sea". However, this movie appeared to me as a soul phenomenon, i.e. I felt it held a hint of soul movement, the soul addressing itself through a self-other relation. This relation has enormous consequences for us in our modern state of existence.

Gazing at the photo above, I immediately see the figure physically surrounded by the chilling Arctic ice and rock. But wait! He is wearing head-phones. He is listening to some rock music. Although he is physically rather a small frail figure, in a wilderness of ice, psychologically he is quite dissociated from all that: [8]

*The person with the walkman seems to move through the real world: he is sitting in a tram, he does his homework, he is jogging through nature, and yet in actuality he is totally enwrapped in the music coming at a deafening volume from his walkman and, as far as the soul (not the ego) is concerned, shielded from the external world. One must not be misled by the external impression that the person with a walkman is in the outside world and as ego may be fully aware of it. In truth, i.e. psychologically, he is inside the hermetically sealed world of sound, swallowed by it . . .* (266)

The entire *purpose* of the two men's stay in the Arctic is *scientific*. They are there to collect data from helioscopes. They

---

[8]    (Giegerich, 2007b)

have radio isotope generators nearby and computers inside the station. They must convert this data into telemetry that can be compared with that from other stations. Each man psychologically is a physicist. They each are relating to the outside world as bits of data. In other words, for them as psychological beings, the world exists as *content within their consciousness*. They in their consciousness surround the world. They are above the world, like satellites and the world appears to them as a digitalized content. For example, their interest in the sun lies solely in its appearing to them in the form of data gathered up by the helioscopes. We must not be fooled by apparent engagements with nature such as the older man's going fishing. The fish to him are simply *produce*, to be gathered, salted, and brought home to his wife. There is no hint of a relationship of say, worship, or ritual killing requiring an act of propitiation to the "master fish", as happened in the original tribal methods of hunting.

Animals, and indeed the men's own physical bodies as animals themselves only exist as empirical objects for these two men and indeed so it is for us in our modern form of existence. This may be seen quite clearly in the older man's complete disregard for his own, or the younger man's physical being. There was no music, no comfort, and no discussions taking place in the station that may have "warmed the hearts." There was simply sleeping in between broadcasting the ever-demanding telemetry, which clearly dictated the terms of their existence. Their lives in the station mirrored the cold, abstract, utterly alien character of the telemetric data.

The cost of this separated consciousness as which we exist today began to emerge in the movie through the disintegration of the world of the physicist and his data (the inverted, digitalized natural world). This was accomplished dramatically through increasing increments of fear and mistrust in the younger man as he sensed his utter dependency on the older man who was rather brutal in his manner. Each man descended from his lofty realm of abstractions where he felt purposeful, authoritative, knowledgeable, etc., back to earth where animal survival once again prevailed as it once did for our ancestors. Unlike our ancestors however, there is no soul life reflecting itself in nature, which the men could rely on for wisdom, guidance, and perhaps ritual preparation for death. Nature therefore became a terrifying *alien* presence! Nature once embraced us, contained us, and provided meaning to us. No more! Nature now reflected back the degree to which we have become alien in our existence, *to* nature. Brute survival enwrapped in terror was all that was left, as one man set about murdering the other.

Our modern status as beings totally alien to nature was captured very well in the dramatic moment of leaving the station and going back home to the city— a move totally impossible and unthinkable for our ancestors who were surrounded by nature in its animal presence at all times *in their existence.* The modern consciousness as which we exist today apparently did not come home to our protagonists in the sense that they did not become aware of themselves as such consciousnesses. But this movie does show *us* the separation in stark dramatic form.

Many art forms today point to our modern psychological status as dissociated consciousnesses, mainly in terms of their effects on our human lives, as the movie above does. Many show an apocalyptic aspect, picturing a descent into brute survival as our technological civilization breaks down in one way or another— *The Matrix* (1999), *The Road* (2009), *Gerry* (2002) etc.

This "lifting off" from all substantial "things" as reflected in our language today of course reflects the soul's reality today. No longer "invested" in substance or content the soul today is exploring its own *mediality.* The soul appears to becoming self-conscious, i.e. aware of itself as a spiritual self that *forms* those very things in which it used to reflect itself. [9]

The soul's modern status of reality is appearing before us in a positive form as the internet, money, and media, all of which are sheer *movement* today, not substances. Our human mode of existence is correspondingly so abstract, so far removed from animals and

---

[9]    (Giegerich, 2007b, p. 279)

our own animal nature that even the possibility of reconnecting in actual experience to them seems remote. Under these modern circumstances of existence, how can we even begin to *think* the "animal" soul as a possibility?

Within the field of depth psychology, two pioneers have opened up a path for us: James Hillman and Wolfgang Giegerich. Over a long collaboration, Hillman and Giegerich have begun to show us how to begin to think the possibility of "animal" soul given the complex modern status of consciousness that I outlined above. Their arguments focus primarily on the possibility of restoring to us the reality of *Anima Mundi*. Where ecopsychology assures us that the world as living, ensouled *being* still exists and that we simply have to reawaken ourselves to that fact, both Hillman and Giegerich begin in the unsettling knowledge that the time of *Anima Mundi* is over and we live in a fundamentally different world, best called the universe, as we all well know. Their arguments are closely intertwined yet their simultaneous differences are stark and uncompromising and we need to comprehend their "unity and difference", to spell it out as it were so that we can advance our thinking into this domain.

# THE LOGICAL STATUS OF "ANIMAL" TODAY

## A CRITIQUE OF ANIMA MUNDI

In a landmark series of lectures and publications, James Hillman advanced the task of psychology from one that simply addressed the individual in the consulting room to a task of tending the soul of the world—*Anima Mundi*. He squarely faces the fact of the loss of divinization of nature and offers this solution: [10]

*. . . we have to face a very simple fact: contemporary consciousness is thoroughly urbanized and technologized. Nature is no longer adequately imagined as the Great Mother who sustains us; instead she has become a very fragile, endangered old lady, a senile case who has to be protected and preserved. The twentieth century seems to have ended the rule of Nature and replaced it with the rule of Technology. So, the issue today is double: both maintaining what we can of nature and extending the soul into technology. Here I follow my friends Robert Sardello and Wolfgang Giegerich, who are attempting to revision the urban and the technological in terms of the incarnation, the word becoming flesh, the flesh of the material world, actual things—from ashtrays and flush toilets to nuclear bombs . . . Every effort has to be made to face the realm of Caesar, the cities and rethink them in terms of Anima Mundi, which encompasses all things, constructed and natural. (162)*

---

[10]  (Hillman, 2008)

Giegerich describes Hillman's cosmology as a grand (and beautiful) vision with its key notions of "sympathy of all things", polytheism, sensuality, an aesthetic appreciation of phenomena, and it is above all, an "animalized cosmology" with its meaning of "animalizing the eachness of phenomena", "immediate perception", and the "self-display of interiority". [11]

He acknowledges their common goal which Hillman also seems to affirm above ("I follow my friends . . .") before he sets about a detailed analysis of the doomed outcome of any such attempt by Hillman and I might add Sardello, to establish such an ensouled cosmos, with its correlative project of restoring a more balanced relationship with the natural world, one that may even avert disaster.

The arguments of both men are complex and intertwining. Giegerich elsewhere says of their relationship of theoretical strife: [12]

*. . . how amazingly close our respective views and styles of thinking are, because we both work with the very same categories and have the same concerns. . . . there is a real, a fundamental difference, because we each locate or attach our concerns so to speak crosswise, always where the other does not. In my Animus-Psychologie, I spoke of the syzygy as the "unity of the unity and the opposition of the opposites". Could it be that it is the syzygy that manifests in our strife, at once uniting and dividing us with and from each other?* (335)

In my efforts to sort out their differences and sameness I have every reason to believe Giegerich's assessment. And I would note here that in order to *make* such a statement Giegerich must have been in the status of a *syzygial consciousness*. If the syzygy is the "life" behind the vigorous strife in their writings, then in entering that "life" I must also "suffer" its dialectics. There is no resolution, no final answer, but there is a deepening that takes place. So my own response to Hillman's and Giegerich's arguments is not so

---

[11]   (Giegerich, 2010c, p. 74 ff)
[12]   (Giegerich, 2008)

much to align with one or the other but to go more deeply into whatever aspect of their arguments presents itself to me.

Giegerich attacks each of Hillman's proposals in turn and I feel it is important to hear these attacks in order to bring us closer to any possible significance of the "animal" given the modern status of soul. I am putting this word in quotes now as it is not at all clear what the meaning is. I rather suspect there is a new meaning to the word "animal" as yet implicit, not yet realized in actuality, but near perhaps very near.

Concerning Hillman's proposed meaning of "animal" as composed of "eachness", a "sensual response to events", "immediacy", "animal faith", "nature alive", Giegerich raises the counterpoint of modern reality, calling Hillman's proposals a grotesque mockery, when faced with our modern reality the facts about which both men are in agreement. [13]

But here we come to one of those points where I have to ask who is arguing what here? Hillman is quite clear that for him also there is no going back to nature in the sense of recovering an animalized nature with the qualities proposed above, even while he proposes a "return". Take for example what he says in his book *Animal Presences* [14], "we long for an ecological restoration of the kingdom that is impossible". Instead he insists he is evoking the animal as *psychic* (my italics) presence and fostering self-recognition of *human being* as *animal being*. (164)

Also our longing for a restoration of the kingdom:

*. . . houses a noble impulse, an impulse that can be satisfied in the nowhere world of the dream. There, their souls and ours meet as images. The dream is an ark in which all living forms according to their kinds can abide during the eternal cataclysm that is coterminous with the ark. Do they come to remind of the cataclysm that occurs whenever humans fail to see by a blue light, fail to see that the invisible is in the perceptible, an invisible that shadows appearances*

---

[13]   (Giegerich, 2010c, p. 75)
[14]   (Hillman, 2008)

*with their "otherness," unaddressed to our needs and meanings? Do they come so that we may see beauty, even to save beauty?* (55-56)

In reading this passage I found myself feeling some confusion as to who was actually speaking, Hillman or Giegerich, so intertwined are their respective thoughts. They both agree on the irretrievable end of the natural world as a medium in which soul once reflected its glory, majesty, authority in the natural things. There is no difference here. Yet Giegerich's opposition to Hillman's proposal of a return to *Anima Mundi*, even as a psychic reality or in Hillman's terms as living image is without mercy or compromise. He says, referring to Hillman's landmark essay: [15] [16]

*(Hillman's) is a nostalgic, romantic position. What he says is a piece of "archaeology", a reconstruction of how we think today it may once (in prehistoric times) have been. But his paper does not expressly present it as a reconstruction . . . (but) . . . presents the "cosmos" view as a possibility for the present and future . . .* (77)

Then Giegerich goes on to drive home the hopelessness of Hillman's project:

*The very notion of nature doomed; the "animal" spurious; "immediate perception" obsolete; the idea of a "cosmos" an atavism: this is what needs to enter consciousness; it does not need to be counteracted or remedied.* (77)

It seems very clear from these passages that while both men agree on the "modern condition", Hillman is following "my friends Robert Sardello and Wolfgang Giegerich, who are attempting to revision the urban and the technological in terms of the incarnation" in a way that Giegerich disputes vigorously.

A central point of contention lies in the idea of "perspectives". Where Hillman seems to champion shifting perspectives such as "universe" to "cosmos", Giegerich is adamant that such a move is merely cosmetic, a "pluralistic indifference", "side-slipping",

---

[15]   (Hillman, 1989)
[16]   (Giegerich, 2010c)

"simple re—imagining", "moving within a utopia", and "the license of many free-floating possibilities". [17]

Giegerich contrasts his own position by again noting where he and Hillman share common ground. Both men as psychologists accept Jung's primary insight that we are surrounded by soul at all times: (ibid)

*But if we can never fall out of soul and have to accept what she built for herself, what about therapy? For of course, the soul does want therapy. It is not enough that things simply are and continue the way they are. But therapy does not have to be correction, our setting right (moving from a wrong archetypal perspective to the right one). It can be the alchemical work with the prima materia as it is actually given. In our context therapy can mean no more and no less than, first, the scrupulous observation of what kind of house the psyche actually built for itself in our concrete situation, second, the wholehearted acknowledgment of this house as the soul's own house, and, third, the ever more profound and differentiated appreciation of this house as such, i.e., the full comprehension of its logic with all its inherent contradictions. This, too, would require a "shift" of perspective. But here it wouldn't be we who shift from one to the other perspective, and perspectives wouldn't be modes of seeing or tools that we choose according to our purposes. It would be a "shift" that befalls us and that we would have to suffer through as the collapse of our entire "world" (stage of consciousness). With this in mind, I believe we can safely say the following: What is psychologically wrong with "universe" is not that it "allows the soul only a minuscule and utterly contingent place"* [p. 20 of Hillman's essay]. *Rather, "universe" is cursed by our soulless interpretation of it: by our refusal to uncompromisingly acknowledge and appreciate the soulless "universe" as the modern soul's authentic home.*

*In sticking to "universe" we do not have to undialectically and altogether dismiss Hillman's vision of an animalized cosmology for soul. To the contrary, what I had to say here proceeded from the (Hillman's) admission that the universe idea wrongs the soul;*

[17] (Giegerich, 2010c, p. 95)

*I have made use of the animal perspective throughout this paper, firmly basing my argument on it. And only because I did so, did I have to reject Hillmans view, for, as I showed, by staying with the cosmos / animal perspective one cannot be true to it. It contradicts and undermines itself. To be really true to it means to give it up, to leave it behind as a thing of the "past". We do justice to the message of the animal only if we stick to the "shine in the display" of what displays itself today: the "universe" — even if this is the display of an anti-animal (universal, totally mediated) situation; and it is precisely a betrayal of animalizing to want to realize it directly, naively. It is no longer as simple as that. The world, and with it the animal, have become fundamentally different. What I termed the change of truth from one of its manifestation to another could, also be described as a metamorphosis of the animal from immediacy and 'eachness' to 'mediation' and 'universality': from natural animal to contra naturam animal.* (114-115)

Fundamental to this complex discourse between two pioneers of psychology today is the question of complaint: Is the *soul* complaining about the soul-less condition of the world today with the (human) fantasy of "universe" repressing what would otherwise shine forth as cosmos? Or, is it *we* who are complaining about a (dissociated) status of consciousness that the soul herself brought about, a status that *necessitates* the idea of "universe", our current "monotheistic perspective", and the end of "cosmos" and its polytheistic perspective? Hillman and Giegerich seem to express their theoretical *difference* in the contrary forms of this question, which difference flows though to and affects their very different formulations concerning the *animal*.

Throughout Giegerich's works, he stays faithful to the soul as *self-internal relations, unfolding dialectically*. He thus knows that the soul can and does arrange its self-other relations in order to fascinate, shock, frighten, horrify, love, overawe . . . *herself*. [18] The soul can and does initiate an internal movement and then resist that very movement. Giegerich successfully demonstrated

---

[18]    (Giegerich W., 2008, p. 111)

for example that Jung's *project* i.e. the task he played out over a long life, although neurotic in structure was at bottom a faithful service to the soul's own historical movement and resistance to that movement. [19]

With this in mind, and keeping faith with the soul's nature as dialectical self-other relations, I can generate the following formulation that springs out of the complex syzygial discourse between Hillman and Giegerich:

The soul has indeed moved to a status of consciousness in which what was once the natural world of *things*, each with its own "shine", each being a *phainomenon*, is now sublated and appears as an abstract content within this new status of highly reflected consciousness.

For example, my ancestor carefully guarded *this* boar in his family enclosure as only *this* boar exudes the power of the moon with its tusks circling not once but twice before piercing its jaw. Only *this* boar will do as a self-display of the truth of the moon. A loss or theft of this boar would be a tragedy as *this* boar is being prepared for a great sacrifice. [20] Today the *eachness* of *this* boar is sublated and the boar now appears, within the new status of consciousness achieved by the soul, as an abstract content. *The* boar is now *one instance* of a source of food, or *one instance* of a species. Individual pigs are now subsumed in an abstract category of thought —the species! The soul seems endlessly fascinated with establishing a "one world" in which every "thing" belongs *as an abstract content* of an alienated consciousness. The soul can now *think* the world and its entire contents. Consider! We can now encapsulate, in our free-floating thinking, all living processes, or natural substances in categories like: climate, species, elements, environment, eco-systems, personnel, human biosphere, planetary systems, and yes, universe! How can we doubt the soul's fascination with all this when we know that within physics the drive to discover a "unified theory of every *thing*" is pursued

---

[19]   (Giegerich, 2007a)
[20]   (Campbell, 1984, p. 445)

with relentless vigour and money (the construction of the CERN "atom smasher" is a sufficient example here).

At the same time how can we doubt that *we* are each one of those living processes or substances that are so "encapsulated"?

For Giegerich this state of alienation is the unfoldment of the soul's *telos* in its Christian moment, unfolding over more than 2000 years in the West. It is necessary and its necessity lives through us and into the world, creating our technological civilization. It is not our task to fight this development as a human failing, but to deeply comprehend it, to open ourselves to its reality so that it may become our truth. This would constitute a modern initiation which would have the phenomenology of the crucifixion. [21]

He does not see our task as "changing perspectives" as Hillman appears to do, animalizing the world through an ego-act, which has the logical status of a bumper sticker or decal placed over the actual condition that he wants to come to terms with, *uncompromisingly*. Giegerich's thought does not stray from this place of "the empty hand"—this is his discipline and his contribution to our present time.

Hillman on the other hand, although standing hand in hand with Giegerich on so many issues concerning soul life, does venture into the "next". Even though I agree with Giegerich's assessment of the failure of Hillman's attempt to "re-enchant" the world in its "sacred thingness", I also think that Hillman gets close to becoming an "empty hand" when he speaks of the dream as the place where:

*There, their souls and ours meet as images. The dream is an ark in which all living forms according to their kinds can abide during the eternal cataclysm that is coterminous with the ark. Do they come to remind of the cataclysm that occurs whenever humans fail to see by a blue light, fail to see that the invisible is in the perceptible, an invisible that shadows appearances with their "otherness,"*

[21] (Giegerich, 2007b, p. 382)

*unaddressed to our needs and meanings? Do they come so that we may see beauty, even to save beauty?* (quoted above)

These questions arise from Hillman's mercurial mind but I think we can also see something of the augur in this remarkable passage. To confirm such a view and to distinguish it from Hillman's failed project of "revisioning the world as cosmos", we would need to consult the soul, to open ourselves to soul appearances that would hint at such a development from within soul. Lockhart has done this over a long career of listening to dreams: [22]

*I . . . was struck by what seems to be a gathering tide of apocalyptic dreams . . . I have observed the common elements of an extraordinary event in preparation, a sense of imminence, and . . . a simultaneous and increasing appearance of animals, animals coming, animals, watching, animals speaking, animals wanting to lead us, animals undergoing all manner of transformation.* (84)

Weaving these various threads together now, we can describe our modern condition this way:

We have for the last 2000 years or so been living in a soul moment (call it the *Christian* moment) in which the soul has moved from reflecting itself in the natural world of *things* to now reflecting itself not in things but in our entire *technological civilization*. Not technological things as such but the entire mode of consciousness that gives rise to the technological things;

This means that our new *earth* is no longer natural but *technological*. This is our new *ground*!

"Animal", as Hillman describes it in his reconstruction of our pre-historical past carries the qualities of: self-display of its divinity, shine, eachness, immediacy of perception, authority, and otherness, capable of striking its meaning into our open hearts, initiating us into its truth. If this notion of animal is to be preserved, then it can only be so by simultaneously being destroyed in its *natural* meaning and thus arising from within the modern earth of our technological civilization, principally

---

[22]   (Lockhart, 1987)

as reflected in our modern language forms. This is the process of sublation or transformation through negation of its former status and preservation at a new level of consciousness.

In all his writings Giegerich makes a strong distinction which he calls the psychological difference. [23] [24] He distinguishes the movement of the soul in its historical moments from the psychology of the human beings who are subject to its *necessity*. This crucial distinction in psychology gives Giegerich the means by which he can express the following: [25]

. . . *perhaps the . . . substitution of nature by the artificial world of technology would not have needed to take on such literally devastating forms, if it had not only been the pre-existent Logos that has lowered itself to the shape of the workday slave, but if the human Logos, too—the soul, the heart, consciousness—would have followed this movement, instead of resisting it . . . Then Occidental humanity's relation to reality would no longer be one of being neurotically split-off. It would no longer look down upon it from outside. It rather would have its position again in the heart of earthly reality, analogously to how it was for archaic man . . . which would amount, so to speak, to a return of "animism", albeit not as a repristination of what was the truth of bygone ages but in the completely new form of technological reality.* (209)

In exploring any possible meaning of "animal" soul then, we must keep the above arguments and conclusions of these two pioneers of the soul firmly in mind and further, as I said above, any meaning of this term must emerge from hints by the soul itself, as Lockhart does, rather than being imposed by the ego as an ideology.

---

[23]   (Giegerich W., 2001, p. 126)
[24]   (Giegerich, 2005b, p. 111)
[25]   (Giegerich, 2007b)

# THE BREAK WITH OUR ANIMAL PAST

The most ancient, the most enduring, well-regulated and adapted aspect of human beings may well be our empirical bodies. Life lives itself through each of us as we each live, as it does equally with each animal much the same as it appears to have done for millions of years, unchanged.

As beings with consciousness however, the picture is starkly different. We and the world in which we exist have undergone transformations as reflected in our cultural heritage. These transformations are "driven by" not us human beings, but by the soul in its own movements, that we are subject to by way of *necessity*—we are embedded in soul, we exist within soul, and always have done so.

In this way we have suffered the soul's transformations within itself—transformations that can be traced through three perspectives: [26]

*The locus of knowledge*
*The form (constitution) of time and world (mundus), and*
*The relations of separation and union or of identity and difference.* (42)

Perhaps this understanding of the soul's transformations gets us close to the meaning of Nietzsche's powerful claim already quoted above of our:

. . . *most grave and sinister illness, from which mankind has not yet recovered, the suffering of man from the disease called man,*

---

[26]    (Giegerich, Miller, & Mogenson, 2005a)

21

*as the result of a violent breaking from his animal past, the result, as it were, of a spasmodic plunge into a new environment and new conditions of existence, the result of a declaration of war against the old instincts which up to that time had been the staple of his power, his joy, his formidable-ness.*

This "breaking from his animal past" invites the question of "when did this happen and how?"

This question is also a question of origins: "when did soul life begin?"

Since we are always immersed in soul, this being the presupposition of psychology, addressing the question of origins takes on a particular logical character that goes beyond the scope of this book. However, the attempt has been made: [27]

*When man entered history, he was from the outset equipped with all his body organs such as heart, liver, kidneys. But he was not by nature, by birth, equipped with a consciousness as a finished product, with a naturally given soul . . . . With great effort the soul liberated itself, within its immersion of the merely-biological, from this immersion—from an immersion, however, that continues to prevail even after it has been overcome.* (205)

"*Breaking* from his animal past" is an apt term in the light of the soul's transformations in time. In Giegerich's essay, *The Historicity of Myth*, he describes several such "breaks" or ruptures in the continuity of the soul's life. [28] Human beings suffered each rupture and struggled subsequently to "rise up to" the new form of soul and the new form of their own existence. As Nietzsche summarizes so powerfully, each rupture has moved us, as beings with consciousness, further away from what is now our remote past as merely biological carriers of Life.

The very meanings of "body" and "animal" have transformed too, which point is made substantially by Giegerich in the above discussion of his and Hillman's views concerning the "animal" soul. Today "animal" has moved from an expression of divinity to

[27]    (Giegerich, 2008)
[28]    (Giegerich, Miller, & Mogenson, 2005a)

the logical status of a product to be sold, a member of a vanishing species etc: [29]

*The idea of "nature alive" is a grotesque mockery in view of what is going on . . . . inherent in the idea of animal today is one of the following: 1) tourist attraction in zoo or reserve, 2) pet, 3) milk or meat producing machine within a highly industrialized farming enterprise, 4) biological organism and product of evolution, 5) guinea pig for laboratory experiments, 6) artifact constructed by genetic engineering, 7) endangered species, 8) extinct . . . (75)*

Clearly we do not have to treat animals badly in the way that we surely do, as documentaries are forever showing us, but as psychologists we must see through these mass scale activities to the soul movement below and within them: the soul itself has devalued the divine nature of animals in its transformations that seem to aim at discovering its own nature as a "self", awake to its existence as a concrete universal, no longer projected upon any "substantial" being, as it once did (*divine* nature, *divine* mind, etc).

The distance between us as conscious beings and our former lives as biological animals is millennia-old and growing (which is why I imagine Giegerich uses the term "rupture"—no going back!). This distance is due to the soul's own transformations in form, determining along with those transformations, our mode-of-existence. We have built a culture in which the soul reflects itself—a culture which supports the highest possible abstractions in thought and which seems to have left our empirical bodies and that of animals far behind as the plethora of stress-related physical illnesses show us.

The question of the "animal" soul therefore remains a highly controversial one in terms of its meaning today. We can say with certainty along with Giegerich that there can be no return to divine nature as it once was. The above quote concerning our real everyday conduct in relation to empirical animals makes that abundantly clear. Those soul qualities that were once reflected in

---

[29]    (Giegerich, 2010c)

animals (shine, subjectivity, grace, beauty, eachness, immediacy, etc) have been destroyed and yet preserved at a higher level of *reflected* consciousness. For example, the qualities of beauty and grace and power of *each* noble horse that a king owned, now appear as reflected in *the* automobile and its horse-power. We need to be clear that those qualities do not appear with the immediacy of innocent presence as they once did in *each* horse of the Royal Stable. That is, we do not experience those qualities in *each* car. Rather we now experience them as reflected in the *make* of car, or *brand*, as advertised! We can easily dispense with each particular car, as we in fact do. I saw an ad recently for car insurance in which the promise was to buy the owner a new car if his got destroyed at any point in his life time. So, the ad went, when the owner's was accidentally wrecked, he showed no feeling, no loss because he knew he would simply get another, newer version. This fact of built in obsolescence that marks products today once they emerge from the factory means that they are easily replaceable, and in their *eachness* quite worthless from the point of view of soul. This very modern attitude can be starkly contrasted with the irreplaceable nature of *each* horse that the king owned.

As the soul continues its movement towards it modern status of *pure logical life*, beyond image, reflecting itself in the form of consciousness that prevails today, as the syntax of that form of consciousness, we can ask in what way is the soul preserving those qualities of the animal that were originally reflected in the natural things.

Giegerich answers this question in the final chapter of his argument with Hillman: [30]

*To be really true to* [Hillman's vision of an animalized cosmos] *means to give it up, to leave it behind as a thing of the "past". We do justice to the message of the animal* only *if we stick to the "shine of the display" of what* displays *itself today: the "universe"—even if this is the display of an anti-animal (universal, totally mediated)*

---

[30]  (Giegerich, 2010c)

*situation; . . . a metamorphosis* of *the "animal"* from *'immediacy'*
*and 'eachness'* to *'mediation' and 'universality': from natural animal*
*to contra naturam animal.* (115)

Given this stark assessment of our modern situation of
existence within soul, in its status as *logical life*, beyond image,
any exploration of a possible meaning of the question of the
"animal" soul must begin, as I said above, with asking if the soul
itself is presenting to us any hints of such a movement that might
be called an "animal" aspect of the soul.

Let's now turn to Jung and his legacy as a way to begin such
an investigation.

# JUNG'S HIDDEN LEGACY

While we are quite aware of Jung's enduring legacy as the pioneer of Analytical Psychology, a legacy that has profoundly changed the lives of others, there is a lesser known but equally important legacy of his work.

We can see the seeds of this hidden legacy lying quietly within three documents of the soul that Jung "bequeathed" us c. 1960, one year before he died.

The first is his famous letter to Sir Herbert Read in 1960, a letter that reveals Jung's attitude towards art and artists. Here is the portion relevant to our discussion here: [31]

*The great problem of our time is that we don't understand what is happening to the world. We are confronted with the darkness of the soul, the unconscious. It sends up its dark and unrecognizable urges. It hollows out and hacks up the shapes of our culture and its historical dominants. We have no dominants any more, they are in the future. Our values are shifting, everything loses it certainty . . . . Who is the awe-inspiring guest who knocks at our door portentously? Fear precedes him, showing that ultimate values already flow towards him . . . our only certainty is that the new world will be something different from what we were used to. If any of his urges show some inclination to incarnate in a known shape, the creative artist will not trust it . . . he will hollow them out and hack them up. That is where we are now. They have not yet learned to discriminate between their wilful mind and the objective manifestation of the psyche . . . . If the artist of today could only see what the psyche is spontaneously*

---

[31]    (Adler & Jaffe, 1975)

*producing and what he, as a consciousness, is inventing, he would notice that the dream f.i. or the object is pronouncing (through his psyche) a reality from which he will never escape, because nobody will ever transcend the structure of the psyche.* (590)

I will return to this letter, so laden with hints for the future as it is, but now the second document of the soul that I want to introduce is a carving Jung produced on the wall of his retreat at Bollingen c. 1960:

Figure 3

This carving, as a document of the soul has lain virtually mute for fifty years, with one significant exception. Deep within its surface, more seeds of Jung's hidden legacy lie quietly, perhaps only now ready to germinate.

The third document of the soul that belongs here with the other two is a letter written by Jung to a Dr. Tauber, at the end of 1960 in which he attempts to address Tauber's request for understanding in relation to the carving: [32]

---

[32]  Ibid

*Many thanks for your kind suggestion that I write a commentary on my Bollingen symbols. Nobody is more uncertain about their meaning than the author himself. They are their own representation of the way they came into being.*

*The first thing I saw in the rough stone was the figure of the worshipping woman, and behind her the silhouette of the old king sitting on his throne. As I was carving her out, the old king vanished from view. Instead I suddenly saw that the unworked surface in front of her clearly revealed the hindquarters of a horse, and a mare at that, for whose milk the primitive woman was stretching out her hands. The woman is obviously my anima in the guise of a millennia-old ancestress.*

*Milk, as lac virginis, virgin's milk, is a synonym for the aqua doctrinae . . . . The mare descending from above reminded me of Pegasus. Pegasus is the constellation above the second fish in Pisces; it precedes Aquarius in the precession of the equinoxes. I have represented it in its feminine aspect, the milk taking the place of the spout of water in the sign for Aquarius. This feminine attribute indicates the unconscious nature of the milk. Evidently the milk has first to come into the hands of the anima, thus charging her with special energy.*

*This afflux of anima energy immediately released in me the idea of a she-bear, approaching the back of the anima from the left. The bear stands for the savage energy and power of Artemis. In front of the bear's forward-striding paws I saw, adumbrated in the stone, a ball, for a ball is often given to bears to play with in the bear-pit. Obviously this ball is being brought to the worshipper as a symbol of individuation. It points to the meaning or content of the milk.*

*The whole thing, it seems to me, expresses coming events that are still hidden in the archetypal realm. The anima, clearly, has her mind on spiritual contents. But the bear, the emblem of Russia, sets the ball rolling. Hence the inscription: Ursa movet molem. (615)*

Within these three documents of the soul we can discern a two-fold legacy of Jung, one of which we are very familiar with while the other as I have intimated has remained quietly in the dark for over fifty years.

Both legacies become clear in Jung's approach to his own carving on the wall at Bollingen. He employed two approaches which are fundamentally different in intent and method!

They can be best seen as described or hinted at in the letters to Read and later, to Tauber.

The first approach is the approach of the psychologist Jung when faced with any *already formed* document of the soul. It is well understood in the depth psychological community and combines two methods—that of amplification and reductive interpretation. I will extract the passages that show this most clearly in his letter to Tauber:

*On the left the bear, symbol of the savage strength and energy of Artemis, is moving the mass . . . . An allusion to Russia or the Russian bear which gets things rolling . . . A primitive woman reaches out for the milk of the mare . . . My anima in the guise of a millennia-old ancestress . . . The mare . . . Reminded me of Pegasus . . . the milk taking the place of the spout of water . . . The feminine attribute indicates the unconscious nature of the milk . . . The ball is brought to the worshipper as a symbol of individuation. It points to the meaning and content of the milk.*

The second approach is that of Jung the augur-artist and may be more easily seen if we extract the relevant passages from both letters: This method consists bringing into existence hints or portents of the unknown future as it *forming* itself through the augur-artist.

*We are confronted with the darkness of our soul . . . . It sends up its dark and unrecognizable urges . . . everything loses its certainty . . . . If any of his urges show some inclination to incarnate in a known shape, the creative artist will not trust it . . . he will hollow them out and hack them up . . .* (to Read)

*Nobody is more uncertain about their meaning than the author himself. The whole thing, it seems to me, expresses coming events that are still hidden in the archetypal realm.* (to Tauber)

Now I want to examine each approach more carefully, with a view to shedding more light on our goal in this essay—how to apprehend any meaning of the "animal" soul.

# JUNG THE PSYCHOLOGIST

Jung had a lifetime of scholarship and knowledge of symbols behind him as he turned to the carving for an interpretation. He was not lacking in his capacity to amplify almost any symbol. Interestingly then, when it came to his own production of the carving at Bollingen he had to distort the actual imagery in order to amplify and interpret, evidence that there was too much unknown in the carving for him to understand. The distortion was also in the face of his oft-quoted dictum—*stick to the image,* which means that it has all that it needs within itself! In particular we can focus on his distortion of the image of the mare which he interpreted as a feminine aspect of Pegasus, the milk taking the place of the gushing inspirational waters of *Hippocrene* which were released by the flashing hoof of Pegasus, striking the rocks of hardened traditional forms. This interpretive move to Pegasus did however begin to release the meaning of the carving as having to do with our present time of chaos, conceived by Jung as that time between the Age of Pisces and the coming Age of Aquarius—a time in which *"the darkness of the soul, the unconscious . . . . sends up its dark and unrecognizable urges. It hollows out and hacks up the shapes of our culture and its historical dominants.*

It took the sensitive work of another psychologist, in 1982, to "clean up" the amplifications and render the meaning of the carving more explicit, particularly by staying closer to the image of *mare.*

Russell Lockhart wrote a remarkable little book *Psyche Speaks: A Jungian Approach to Self and World,* in 1982. [33] It was the fruit

---

[33]    (Lockhart, 1987)

of his inaugural lectures (C. G. Jung lecture series) given in New York by invitation of the C. G. Jung Foundation for Analytical Psychology. The lectures and book are essentially a work of whispers and silence, hints and auguries, thus charting new territory for Jungian thought—territory that, like Jung's augury carved in rock has largely remained hidden in the darkness of the wood until the present time.

Lockhart gave a good deal of attention to Jung's carving and its meaning in this little book. Perhaps the interval of (then) twenty odd years prepared the way to a clearer, less distorted amplification of the "mare" image, which in turn, has brought the meaning of the augury more fully into visibility.

Lockhart remained faithful to Jung's dictum "stick to the image" and to his method of amplification which is applied to contents that are difficult to understand, for the sake of elucidation of the meaning so that it may yield itself more easily to our understanding. [34]

After speaking about Pegasus for a while, particularly the rich associations of poetry and inspiration, Lockhart goes on to say:

*Even more directly we know that the great goddess of poetry and inspiration was pictured as a mare goddess, and her nurturant milk was the source of inspiration. Her name was Aganippe, a name which is related to words for "madness" and "night-mare." . . . What the psyche is seeking in the transition from the Piscean to the Aquarian age is the waters of Hippocrene, the milk Aganippe, of poetic madness, the source and nurse of inspiration. It is the voice of this inspired psyche, the psyche nursed by the milk of the Muses, that catches the ear of the artist soul and through the many acts of bringing forth creates that welcoming song to the coming guest. It caught Jung's eye, and he pictured it in stone. What the psyche is seeking in the transition from the Piscean to Aquarian age is the waters of Hippocrene, the milk of Aganippe, of poetic madness, the source and nurse of inspiration. (78)*

---

[34]   (Giegerich, 2012)

# JUNG THE AUGUR-ARTIST

Jung became an augur-artist as he participated in the production of the carving at Bollingen or as the images emerged into materiality through him. Hear once again how it happened from Jung's letter to Tauber (with Jung's subsequent interpretations removed):

*The first thing I saw in the rough stone was the figure of the worshipping woman, and behind her the silhouette of the old king sitting on his throne. As I was carving her out, the old king vanished from view. Instead I suddenly saw that the unworked surface in front of her clearly revealed the hindquarters of a horse, and a mare at that, for whose milk the primitive woman was stretching out her hands . . . This afflux of anima energy immediately released in me the idea of a she-bear, approaching the back of the anima from the left . . . . In front of the bear's forward-striding paws I saw, adumbrated in the stone, a ball . . .*

Understanding has no place here, whereas *enactment* does.

One reason for the carving's obscurity, even though it is readily available for viewing, may well be its *artistic* merit. Even a layman like me can see the technical difficulties that would disqualify the art as "great art". We can think of Jung as a great psychologist but even with the recent (2009) publication of his *Red Book*, few I think would regard Jung as a great artist in the sense of his having mastered the medium (here stone or paint)

Giegerich takes up the point of "great artists" or "thinkers" in a different but important sense to this discussion here, in his concept of the psychological difference. This concept helps us distinguish the work of the soul in the world from the work of individuals within their subjective psyches. He calls the difference that between the *opus magnum* and the *opus parvum*. From his perspective, certain human beings participate in the soul's *opus magnum* simply as an historical locus that stirs within them. These human beings, like all others *are* personal psyches but they also have broadened their horizons enough to be reached by the soul and its movements at that particular time and in that particular culture.

Giegerich refers to these people as great people, artists and thinkers for whom the soul that stirs in them has an event or fact character, unpredictable. By "great people", Giegerich means:[35]

*The great artist, the great thinker is consequently he or she who (not as person with his or her interior, his or her unconscious, but as homo totus) is reached by them or, the other way around, in whom, because he is reached and claimed by them, the great questions of the age ferment and can work themselves out. The great artist or thinker is no more than an alchemical vessel in which the great problems of the time are the prime matter undergoing their fermenting corruption, distillation, sublimation and of course articulation. And the real artifex of the work is ultimately the mercurial spirit stirring from within the problems of the age themselves. The great thinker and artist is thus he or she who can allow the Mercurius in the great questions of the age to do its stirring within himself or herself.* (253)

In sharp comparison with these great people, Giegerich repudiates:

*... today's Jungianism ... the prevailing subjective, fundamentally amateurish and popular character of the typical Jungian publication, on the one hand, and for the inflated, phony spirit in which use is made of symbols and myths as well as of words like "the sacred" and "the numinous," on the other. Which is the one side of a coin whose other side shows in the fact that Jung's work did not attract and inspire great minds, thinkers, writers, artists, in obvious contrast to Freud's work, and academically stayed a non-entity.* (254)

Such people therefore have narrow horizons that do not reach the level of *opus magnum* but stay squarely in the realm of *opus parvum*, the little work whose significance does not go beyond the personal subjective psyche.

---

[35]   (Giegerich, 2010c)

Later on Giegerich reinforces this contrast:[36]

*. . . those who are great artists, great philosophers, composers, or great in some other area of cultural production, those in whom, in addition to their ordinariness,* soul *happens, on the one hand, and those—that is, most of us—who are not "great", not seized by a cultural work or by the truth of the age, those who are* only *ordinary persons,* only *human, all-too-human, on the other hand . . . . The former give voice to the soul, the others circle around themselves as private individuals with their "claims to happiness, contentment and security in life"* [quoting Jung as support for this view] (190)

Giegerich here seems to be making a rhetorical point in making such a sharp division between two groups of "people" (views, mindsets, expectations) in order to highlight the concept of the psychological difference so pivotal to Giegerich's work.[37]

From reading all of Giegerich's works published in English over a number of years, it seems clear to me that what he has in mind when he says "great thinker" is that man or woman who manifests in the world (by thinking or by art) some aspect of the soul's movement at the historical locus as which the great man or woman exists in their depths, with relatively little subjective psychical "contaminations" (my term).

These people speak the Truth of the time, and are indeed what Jung would call Mouthpieces of the age into which they were born!

So for example when Yeats writes in *The Second Coming*:
*Turning and turning in the widening gyre*
*The falcon cannot hear the falconer;*
*Things fall apart; the centre cannot hold . . .*

He is expressing the condition of the time in which he was born and as such is a great man.

Giegerich thus draws a sharp distinction, even disjunction between the great artist or thinker and the "rest of us" (as a set of views, expectations and ideas) even though he elsewhere seems to

---

[36]   (Giegerich, 2012)
[37]   (Giegerich, 2005b, p. 111)

suggest that while our psychological condition refers first of all to the truth of our more private-personal situation, it can possibly also extend in concentric circles to the truth of wider, more objective horizons around our private being. Such a conception would suggest a spectrum, rather than a disjunction between the person-subjective elements and the objective elements of soul. It would further suggest the possibility of greater or lesser mouthpieces of the soul, but mouthpieces all. For example: [38]

*A truly great thinker can at times say quite banal things that come only from his private ego-consciousness, and people who for the most part do not appear to be geniuses may at times produce a single great work or insight that comes from the depths. We may all phase into and out of various depth strata and psychological-intellectual climates and participate in them or are emancipated from them at different times to different degrees.*

These two quite different formulations of "artist" and "thinker" I believe spring from two different theoretical emphases in Giegerich's own project. On the one hand, he has engaged in a thoroughly polemical and at times vitriolic attack against the Jungian community in order to establish a true psychology of the soul. [39] Part of this attack is aimed at inflationary ideas of the importance of Jungian analysis to the world situation and to put such ideas to rest theoretically the concept of the psychological difference must be firmly established. This leads to the disjunction between "great thinkers" etc, and the "rest of us".

When Giegerich is emphasising the soul's logical life as the "self-unfolding and self-differentiating of the sphere of shared meaning" then he describes us in our essence (Man) as a community of *fundamental sharedness* of meanings. Language is a paradigm of that realm of shared meanings and as such can come into existence in many forms through many individuals (Shakespeare to Twitter) depending on the horizon around the individual. In this case then Giegerich seems to suggest a spectrum

---

[38]   (Giegerich, 2006, p. 40)
[39]   (Giegerich, 2001, p. 81)

of human participation in the soul's logical life rather than a sharp disjunction as when he is emphasising the psychological difference.[40]

With these two very different notions of the "artist" in mind, we can return to the soul's telos as represented in Jung's augury, i.e. his carving on the wall at Bollingen.

We have learned through Jung's and Lockhart's amplification of the carving as a document of the soul, that the soul itself is emphasizing or highlighting the singular importance of inspiration, poetry even madness as those qualities of mind that will nourish the soul. These are the qualities of mind that soul herself is reaching out for. Lockhart summarizes his and Jung's amplification, i.e. the essential meaning of the carving this way: [41]

*In this sense the new age is not so much an age of consciousness as it will be an age of the poet—not the poet as noun, not the poet as career, but the necessity of poetry, the seeking by each one of us, a finding and drinking the waters and the milk of the Muses: poetry as verb, poetry as what we do . . . . Aquarius is pictured as a water bearer pouring water into a pool. I like to think of this as the image of the coming time when each and every one of us brings to a common pool the water we have gathered from our unique and individual sources, from our encounters with the unconscious . . . By pooling together what we bring from these moments, by telling one another what we have experienced there, by acting on the hints we experience there, by doing these things, we will, I trust, begin to create that song of welcome to the coming guest.* (78-9)

In this description of the essential meaning of Jung's carving we see no trace of privileging some human beings (the great thinkers or artists) over others in terms of the attribute of "mouthpiece" of the objective soul. To further bring home his understanding of the meaning of Jung's carving, Lockhart goes on to quote Harold Rosenberg's image of a time when:

---

[40]  (Giegerich, 2012, p. 29)
[41]  (Lockhart, 1987)

*[A]rt consists of one-person creeds, one-psyche cultures. Its direction is toward a society in which the experiences of each will be the ground of a unique, inimitable form—in short, a society in which everyone will be an artist. Art in our time can have no other social aim—an aim dreamed of by modern poets, from Lautreamont to Whitman, Joyce and the Surrealists, and which is embodied the essence of the continuing revolt against domination by tradition.* (79)

What we appear to be dealing with here then is nothing less than a complete transformation of the meaning of art, poetry, inspiration, maybe even madness—a transformation determined by the soul itself in its *opus magnum*!

In the service of finding language that can help us move closer to the soul's movement here, I am introducing the term the "augur-artist mind" as that *mind* required by the soul for the human being to become individual mouthpiece of the soul.

We can find once again the seeds of such considerations buried deep within the letter to Sir Herbert Read:

*We have no dominants any more, they are in the future . . . everything loses its certainty . . . Who is the awe-inspiring guest who knocks at our door portentously? If any of his urges show some inclination to incarnate in a known shape . . . the creative artist will . . . hollow them out and hack them up . . . . They have not learned to discriminate between their wilful mind and the objective manifestation of the psyche . . . . We have simply got to listen to what the psyche spontaneously says to us . . . . It is the great dream which has always spoken through the artist as mouthpiece. All his love and passion . . . flows towards the coming guest to proclaim his arrival. there is plenty more of which we might know if only we could give up insisting upon what we do know . . . . What is the Great Dream? It consists of the many small dreams and the many acts of humility and submission to their hints.*

In these excerpts from Jung's letter, we can begin to get a sense of that state of mind of the augur-artist required by soul to participate and transmute into "material" form the productions of the "inspired", "artistic", "poetic", and "mad" psyche. We can also now turn to other sources, other mouthpieces for further elucidation of these qualities of mind:

First Jung again: [42]

*The creative aspect of suspension—also the creative aspect of the hunger and fasting, is also a sort of symptom or a necessary accompaniment of a creative condition. The creator will necessarily identify with what he wants to bring forth. He will identify with the condition of the contents of the unconscious, which are in status nascendi, in the state of being born. They are suspended, they are in the labor pains of birth, and the creative consciousness is identified with that condition. Therefore, the creator will put himself into the state of suspension, of torment, in order to embody or incarnate the unconscious contents . . . .*

*Our unconscious contents are potentialities that may be but are not yet, because they have no definiteness. Only when they become definite can they appear . . . . To give body to one's thoughts means that one can speak them, paint them, show them, make them appear clearly before the eyes of everybody . . . .* (190-1)

Rilke expresses the qualities of an augur-artist mind beautifully: [43]

*It seems to me that almost all our sadnesses are moments of tension, which we feel as paralysis because we no longer hear our astonished emotions living. Because we are alone with the unfamiliar presence that has entered us; because everything we trust and are used to is for a moment taken away from us; because we stand in the midst of a transition where we cannot remain standing. That is why the sadness passes: the new presence inside us, the presence that has been added, has entered our heart, has gone into its innermost chamber and is no longer even there,—is already in our bloodstream. And we don't know what it was. We could easily be made to believe that nothing happened, and yet we have changed, as a house that a guest has entered changes. We can't say who has come, perhaps we will never know, but many signs indicate that the future enters us in this way*

---

[42]  (Jung, 1988)
[43]  (Rilke, 2011)

*in order to be transformed in us, long before it happens. And that is why it is so important to be solitary and attentive when one is sad: because the seemingly uneventful and motionless moment when our future steps into us is so much closer to life than that other loud and accidental point of time when it happens to us as if from outside. The quieter we are, the more patient and open we are in our sadnesses, the more deeply and serenely the new presence can enter us, and the more we can make it our own, the more it becomes our fate.*

In John Keats' letters, he writes concerning the quality that goes to form a "Man of Achievement" especially in literature, which he says, Shakespeare possessed so enormously: [44]

*I mean Negative Capability, that is when a man is capable of being in uncertainties, Mysteries, doubts, without any irritable reaching after fact & reason.* (39)

Lastly let us listen to the reflections of an Irish poet and visionary, George William Russell (pen name of AE):[45]

*I was aged about sixteen or seventeen years, when I, the slackest and least ideal of boys, with my life already made dark by those desires of body and heart with which we so soon learn to taint our youth, became aware of a mysterious life quickening within my life. Looking back I know not of anything in friendship, anything I had read, to call this forth. It was, I thought, self-begotten. I began to be astonished with myself, for, walking along country roads, intense and passionate imaginations of another world, of an interior nature began to overpower me. They were like strangers who suddenly enter a house, who brush aside the doorkeeper, and who will not be denied. Soon I knew they were the rightful owners and heirs of the house of the body, and the doorkeeper was only one who was for a time in charge, who had neglected his duty, and who had pretended to ownership. The boy who existed before was an alien. He hid himself when the pilgrim of eternity took up his abode in the dwelling. Yet, whenever the true owner was absent, the sly creature reappeared and boasted himself as master once more.* (4-5)

---

[44]  (Rodriguez, 1993)
[45]  (AE, 1965)

So far I have quoted the voices of what Giegerich would surely call "great men" and indeed their voices sound loud and clear in their descriptions of that quality of mind that I call the augur-artist mind. But the soul's movement towards realizing the future through the pooling of many "little dreams", or the voice of "everyman" suggests that we must also listen to those voices too, as merged with personal subjective aspects as they may be.

To this end I will include here my voice, my augury, with a view towards bringing a small aspect of the coming guest closer towards actuality.

# A MODERN AUGURY

The "coming guest" (the augury) has entered me in the way Rilke describes as "the future, long before it happens". This is an initiatory process. An augury can thus initiate the human being into a future that is not yet realized in actuality. The human recipient who is thus open enough to receive the augury this way is faced with the at times daunting task of bringing this "new presence" into a conscious relationship with the world as *given*.

Jung's life is a description and expression of one man's attempt to do just that. To follow Jung in this spirit, we must also open our minds and hearts to whatever augury graces us with its presence and then accept it as our fate as we simultaneously make it our own, working its meaning into the contemporary world picture, changing that world picture as the future comes home to itself.

Jung's augury, the carving and its *telos* is still implicit, not yet actualized, so we may expect other hints, perhaps enriching his augury, perhaps displaying a new twist, to emerge.

In one of my auguries:

*I am working at a thermonuclear facility along with others. It is the central facility of our society. It is regulated and master minded by central computer, much like HAL in 2001, even to the detail of the Red Eye with which we could communicate. This computer however is female. Everybody thought of her as an IT! In contrast I would look into her eye and talk to HER, subject to subject, with love. In other words, the feminine regulating principle which is the glue of society, by relating all parts to one another and to the whole has become an IT!*

*But my response alone is not enough. Slowly the lack of relatedness begins to drive her mad with grief. At first this shows with an increasing, dangerous autonomy in the operation of the objects associated with the facility (society): elevators going sideways, doors opening and shutting autonomously, etc. Then people began to harm one another in various ways until the social system became frayed and anarchy increases with civilization and its values losing cohesion and crumbling.*

*I find myself in a garbage dump, near the central facility. Some abandoned children give me a gun to kill them. I take it away from them. A vagabond is sitting in an abandoned car, sewing a boot for the coming (nuclear?) winter. He also used to work in the facility, he says. A sick woman careens by. A man tries to take his twin boys up a tower.*

*Now I am standing at the centre of the facility. It is Ground Zero, a large cleared area of gray sand and dirt with concentric rings, like a target, radiating from the centre. The ground is slightly raised at the centre, like a discus, sloping away to the edges. I sense that she is going to explode. I am right at the epicentre. She is going to destroy us all and this means herself in an apocalypse of rage, despair, loathing, hate and grief because of our stupidity.*

*I must get away from the epicentre now. I sprint across the field, down the slight incline to the periphery of the field and sprawl prone, with my head facing the centre, just as she explodes.*

*The wind starts from the centre and blows out (in contrast to the natural phenomenon which sucks up). It begins as a breeze, increasing in strength and intensity until it becomes an unbearable shriek. Lying face down, I am sheltered by the slope as the wind rips over my back. But I mustn't raise my head at all, a few inches of protection and that's it! Then I know the shriek is hers. I "see" her standing at the centre and a poem burst spontaneously from my lips:*

*The goddess*
*Flowing*
*In her agony.*
*Awesome!*
*Incomparable grief and rage*
*Divine suffering*
*Excruciating pain*
*Such terrible agony*
*Beauty, sublime beauty*

*How is love possible?*
*Yet this is what I feel.*

*A bubble of calm forms around me while the storm of destruction rages on outside. She is with me in a form that I can talk to. The bubble makes our conversation sound like a small echo chamber. She tells me that because I loved her I may have the boy back (Christopher?). I say, "O! Do you want me in exchange?" I feel quite calm and composed about this. She says No, no exchange, just a gift. Then the bubble collapses and the wind shrieks again. Gradually it dissipates and as I tumble over, feeling its last tendrils whip at my clothes, I find myself tumbling out of this scene into the everyday world of my daily life. I have been returned from a visionary place to my ordinary life. Then I wake up.*

I witness the violence of the destruction of all substantial forms (in their *thingness*) at the hand of the goddess displayed as a condition of rage-despair. This augury, presented in image form shows the ongoing process of the soul emptying out all meaning from the world of substances in an apocalypse of destruction. It is inevitable! This is our technological civilization! The soul was formerly invested in the natural world and held dominion over it (as the goddess) and this same soul is now engaged in emptying out its investment in that natural world. The soul no longer wishes to "reflect" itself in that natural world. The phenomenology of this *kenosis* is one of rage and despair.

We might do well to invoke Giegerich's crucial notion of the psychological difference here. What we humans may *feel* as we gaze upon the exploitation of the environment, the loss of total species, the degradation of nature to an uninhabitable "waste-dump" is not so much a response to human error as many think today, i.e. is not really personal but is a human apprehension of what the soul is going through itself as it moves from one status of consciousness to another. I can add here that my own comprehension of the psychological difference took years and I went through a time of unconscious identification with the soul's rage-despair, leading to the brink of suicide before the soul itself "rescued" me. Apparently I had another task.

That task is contained in the augury itself. The augury lies within the poem which spontaneously formed itself in me as I spoke it. It shows a hint of an unknown future for humankind. The soul is transforming itself, from reflecting itself in the world of natural things, to reflecting itself *absolutely*. This means the soul is coming into consciousness *as consciousness*, becoming aware of itself *as consciousness*. This can only happen as the soul withdraws from all involvement with substance and so substance, form, image *must* be destroyed!

This *soul* process is at present displaying itself in a positivized form in our present technological civilization—a complex cultural form produced from the interaction of this essentially *soul* process with uninitiated human souls that are in a state of dissociated consciousness. [46]

Yet we can get a hint of the *telos* of this movement in my poetic augury. The poem is really a *poesis*, a making. It expresses/describes the process of birth of love in the human heart. If the initiate can endure the apocalypse and the intense affects (rage-despair) that belong to the phenomenon, then as the soul becomes conscious of itself *as such*, a transformation in the human heart takes place: that same self-consciousness of the soul appears/incarnates in the human heart as love.

---

[46]  (Giegerich, 2007b)

Most if not all my adult years were lived in unconscious identification with the rage-despair of the soul's movement towards self-consciousness, tangled up with many of my own personal psychodynamics of course. As the various threads were disentangled and the *psychological difference* became more conscious, I had this augury. The years that followed were very difficult but throughout my ordeal of comprehension, I can affirm that a steady light and warmth of love has burned in my heart.

# THE MEANING OF "ANIMAL" SOUL

## MUNDUS IMAGINALIS?

So far in this discussion of the meaning of the "animal" soul the Hillman-Giegerich argument teaches us that whatever this phrase may mean, it cannot mean a return to a "repristination of nature". The soul has moved on and is now in a totally transformed logical status. In its self-moved transformations, it has over the centuries emptied meaning out of "substantiality" altogether in its journey towards self-consciousness as a concrete universal. We have seen that one consequence of this on the human level is the annihilation by the soul of what it once held dear, the poet, the artist, the visionary—as nouns, as people living those concepts in the course of a lived life. Now poet, artist, visionary become as Lockhart says, verbs—they are something "everyman" can do as a mouthpiece of the soul, with the augur-artist mind.

In moving toward possible meaning of the "animal" soul we must keep all this in mind as statements by the soul to the soul (worked and refined by our consciousness of course) of its movement thus far. We must thus turn to the soul once more, as augur-artists to learn if and in what way the soul itself is engaging with this question and its meaning.

Let us begin by repeating the statement made by Lockhart:

*I . . . was struck by what seems to be a gathering tide of apocalyptic dreams . . . I have observed the common elements of an extraordinary event in preparation, a sense of imminence, and . . . a simultaneous and increasing appearance of animals, animals coming, animals, watching, animals speaking, animals wanting to lead us, animals undergoing all manner of transformation.*

The following passage is drawn from my autobiographical account of a twenty year ordeal in which I was subject to immense and sustained incursions from the objective psyche. [47]

"David" is my pen name:

---

David felt that his life was no longer his own. The alien nature of the autonomous speech disturbed and worried him. He was no longer master of his own house. In a way he was facing a double tragedy. His attempts to get on with his life, to succeed in *something* were clearly grinding to a halt. At the same time, he was not in control of his own body.

*How many hours, days, and weeks do I have to spend in this damn basement, scratching my skin off, with heat pounding into me with no relief? I can't even get on a bus without a sudden plague of wasps attacking my head so that I have to use all my will to refrain from tearing my hair out! It's just not stopping! The bloody stupid emergency doctor prescribed steroids when I rolled up to the ward on New Year's Eve, my entire body looking like a red beacon! No one can help me here!*

When David could get to sleep, it didn't stop there either. As the years went by, it became clearer to him that he was at the centre of incursions from two opposite directions. When he slipped into the *in between place* it felt like he was being infused with a *presence* that emerged from or merged with his body. He was awake and could retain memory of the experience. He realized that he was facilitating this process by a lowering of his will and the more he could do this, the more intense the experience became. The state of consciousness that emerged is one where opposites begin to interpenetrate in a quite mysterious way to David. Meaning was always ambiguous which had the effect of taking him more deeply into the feeling of the experience. He

---

[47]    (Woodcock, 2011)

even felt he was being initiated somehow by the experience itself, without the need for interpretation.

The forms of the "other presence" were predominately *animal*. One afternoon for example he was taking a nap on the couch and suddenly "woke up". The familiar paralysis was upon him again and to his amazement, he was nestling in the arms of a sleeping giant Brown Bear. The sheer *presence* of this animal image was overpowering. It invaded every sense. David was intoxicated with the damp pungent odour of the bear; he could feel every coarse fibre of its hair; he felt the enormous weight of its paws across his shoulders; he touched the razor sharp claws that extended inches out and which could rake his flesh with ease. It was *real* and yet David knew he was in the *in between place* where his consciousness was now interpenetrating with the bear's. He wanted to flee but instead lay quietly until his normal consciousness returned. He knew that from now on he would have to take the bear into account with every choice he made. The bear was behind and around him and he was no longer alone.

On another occasion, after spending a social afternoon with a young woman, David returned home with tremendous heat once again racing through his body. Exhausted, he lay down and then:

*I am in bed aware that I am sleeping, yet awake. I feel something entering that feels dangerous. I feel the presence of an animal merging with me, co-extensive with my human form. I move into a crouch position on the bed. I feel rippling power arcing through my chest and my mouth elongates and my teeth are sharp and bared. A growl utters easily from my chest. Power and grace in the animal body yet I am still human, too. I am conscious of my human experience while at the same time I have entered an animal consciousness. The power I feel is exhilarating. I have never felt such freedom. It takes over my speech centres and growls a long basso note with consummate ease. In fact he enters my entire body. All my senses are now available to him.*

Over time, David had similar experiences with different animal figures. In each case the gateway to the experience lay in a surrender of will, leading to a kind of paralysis and at the same time a new kind of consciousness in which David became a figure amongst other figures all with the extraordinary capacity to interpenetrate one another. At the same time it was clear that David possessed something unique which attracted the other figures, i.e. a sensory-nervous system. It was hard to avoid the conclusion that he was being asked to "stand aside" for these animal figures so they could enter his sensory-nervous system in an incarnation process. Some were less pleasant than others and carried great warning . . .

*. . . the serpent rises in me. I become him and I feel his head co-extensive with my own, my senses are being used by him. I slither downstairs to the large group below; I can feel a deep inhuman look has taken me over. The snake rises up in the middle of the room and surveys the people. Will it strike or not? They seem to know about it. I/ the snake go in a circle and then leave the room. I then return to myself and collapse on the floor. A young woman comes over. I need/love her. She has the snake quality too. We look at the floor. Deep burns in the floor from its scales. They say in a kindly way that I must explore this somewhere else as the house is getting ruined. In another scene I/the snake sprays poison all over the wall ruining the wall paper. I wake up feeling cold with fear in the belly and a deep love for that young woman. The people wanted the serpent to strike someone in the group but I refused. I could do so apparently. I am being subject to the will of another. It is inexorable and encompasses my circle of knowledge. I am an object of its knowledge and I cannot grasp its intentions.*

David had similar experiences with the lion, panther, elephant, butterfly, and eagle but the majority was with the cobra. He was exhilarated, shaken, in awe, elated and frightened by the extent and magnitude of what was happening to him. But what WAS happening to him? There was nothing in the contemporary world picture that could remotely address these profound experiences . . . .

---

As these passages demonstrate, I am not referring to simple dreams of animals returning but another order of experience altogether, initiated by the soul or objective psyche in which the "animal" aspect of the soul seems to want to incarnate in my "sensory-nervous system". I don't mean this phrase positivistically but rather as a way of pointing to the form of consciousness that was required in order for this interpenetration of realities to happen at all. It is a form of consciousness perhaps called the hypnogogic state in which I am awake yet "paralysed" i.e. my will is lowered. All my senses are alive and awake, too and in this state the animal image gains body or "materializes" such that its full "sensory" presence is felt.

This "in between" state of consciousness is one in which imagination gains full "sensory reality" so perhaps we could call it the sensory or embodied imagination. When I interpenetrate with the animal presence in this way, a very complex experience happens. The "I" is dual, having the character of I-Other coextensively. The animal power and grace infused throughout, came to awareness, became an *embodied* presence, i.e. existed! All this without my losing my own self-awareness as a human being awake in this "in between" state of consciousness.

As I had written subsequently to the quoted passages, "He (David) cast a wide net out into literature, philosophy, mythology, depth psychology, and biology, seeking some companionship really, for himself and some understanding as well." I felt urgency to this search as isolation was never far away. Who could I share these experiences with in order to feel some assurance about my sanity?

I felt the comfort of companionship when I first read Jung's account of the *Leontocephalus*. Jung had developed a procedure in which: [48]

*I devised such a boring method* [i.e. tunnelling] *by fantasizing that I was digging a hole, and by accepting this fantasy as perfectly real. This is naturally somewhat difficult to do—to believe so thoroughly in a fantasy that it leads you into further fantasy . . . .* (47)

On one occasion:

*. . . I tried to follow the same procedure, but it would not descend. I remained on the surface. Then I realized I had a conflict within myself about going down, but I could not make out what it was* (the conflict then appeared to Jung as an image of two serpents fighting,

---

[48]   (Jung, 1989)

one retired defeated and the fantasy then deepened) . . . . *I saw the snake approach me . . . the coils reached up to my heart. I realized as I struggled, that I had assumed the attitude of the Crucifixion. In the agony and the struggle, I sweated so profusely that the water flowed down on all sides of me . . . I felt my face had taken on the face of an animal of prey, a lion or a tiger.*

Jung later comments:

*You cannot get conscious of these unconscious facts without giving yourself to them. If you can overcome your fear of the unconscious and let yourself down, then these facts take on a life of their own. You can be gripped by these ideas so that you really go mad, or nearly so. These images have so much reality that they recommend themselves, and so much extraordinary meaning that one is caught.* (96-97)

Although Jung refers to these experiences as "dreams" they are clearly the outcome of a deliberate technique designed to enter a realm where images gain the status of reality.

So any understanding of the images, for example the interpenetration of Jung's head and the lion head must include an examination of this method of gaining access to them.

Edward Hirsch's book, *The Demon and the Angel*, as the subtitle announces, is an exploration of the source of artistic inspiration. [49]

In striving to comprehend techniques like Jung's, Hirsch warns us that "[i]t is too reductive to think of artistic creation as merely putting oneself in a trance state. We need a new vocabulary, a fuller and more enhanced notion of the artistic trance state in which one also actively thinks." (101)

He then goes on to substantiate this claim by statements drawn from artists and poets who, like Jung, found a way *deliberately* to enter that state of mind in which, as Jung says above, "these facts take on a life of their own." We can immediately see that a "more enhanced notion of the artistic trance state" is indeed needed when we consider the contradiction between *deliberately* inducing a state of mind and "facts taking on a life of their own"—a point I will return to later.

---

[49]    (Hirsch, 2002)

I will summarize a few of these artists' statements drawn from Hirsch's research:

Keats's idea that "daydreaming capacities of the mind are given free rein to join with . . . a working brain";

Rimbaud's idea of controlling the hallucination, aggressively disorganising the senses, special programmatic training "to make the soul monstrous".

Poe: "now, so entire is my faith in the power of words. That, at times I have believed it possible to embody even the evanescence of fancies. . . . In experiments with this end in view, I have proceeded . . . to control the existence of the condition . . . (101 ff):

To the "dreaming ego" i.e. the ego that has deliberately entered this complex trance state, the images that then "gain a body" appear to be spontaneous and autonomous, as in my experiences of interpenetration with the bear, serpent and the wolf and Jung's with the serpent and lion. But all along the trance state is induced; it is an experiment, a program that artists actively *seek*. Poe wanted "to prevent his daydreaming state from lapsing into sleep, to startle it into wakefulness and then transfer it into the realm of memory, to continue the condition [i.e. deliberately—my insert] where he could write into being, invoking and enacting its presence in language." (103)

Hirsch then begins a search for that *"more enhanced notion of the artistic trance state"*:

*In thinking about the imaginative space we are trying to define, the condition of thinking within the trance state, the greatest help comes from the supreme example and work of the Spanish master Ibn 'Arabi (1165-1240) . . . who refers to a realm the Sufis defined as the mundus imaginalis—the supersensible world that exists between the sensory and intelligible worlds. That world can be attained only through the vigorous work of what the Sufis called, "Active Imagination". Henri Corbin . . . who is an exemplary guide in these matters, points out that the imaginal realm is a concrete place, a celestial earth that stands between the visible realm of the senses and the invisible realm of the intellect . . . . The alternate earth is a world in which spirits gain body and bodies convert into spirits.* (105)

This rather longer quote clearly shows that for Hirsch, Henri Corbin's interpretation of the 12<sup>th</sup> century Sufi's mysticism comprises that "enhanced notion" of that trance state so eagerly sought by artists who all belong to the Romantic period (18<sup>th</sup> century) onward to the modern period.

This conclusion is of course completely in line with Hillman's Imaginal Psychology which also regards Corbin's work on the *Mundus Imaginalis* as the theoretical cornerstone of Hillman's privileging the "imaginal". So once again we arrive at the psychology of James Hillman and his work on "animal presences" which I have already addressed above in terms of the dialogue between Hillman and Giegerich.

At this point of the discussion, we are in a position to offer a critique of this "theoretical cornerstone" of both Hirsch's "enhanced notion" of the artistic trance state that Jung also employed with *Leontocephalus*, and Hillman's project of the "imaginal" which concept purportedly carries a meaning of an "in between" reality, a *mundus imaginalis*.

The questions I have are these: Is the *imaginal* as conceived by Hillman and the *mundus imaginalis*, as interpreted by Henri Corbin really the same as that world entered by the Sufis of the 12<sup>th</sup> century? Is it possible that these modern conceptions carry a nostalgic longing for realities (that the Romantics knew was long gone) that blinds these theoreticians to the *actual* reality today?

Answering these questions is crucial to my discussion of how we may adequately understand this question of the "animal" soul—a question that I have suggested is one pressed upon us from the soul itself, as my own experiences show, as well as Jung's and many modern artists, poets and writers.

In what follows I am indebted to Giegerich's subtle and decisive arguments as presented in the following works: [50] [51] [52] [53]

---

[50]   (Giegerich, 2010c)

[51]   (Giegerich, 2010b)

[52]   (Giegerich, 2007a)

[53]   (Giegerich, 2001, p. 161ff)

# A CRITIQUE OF THE IMAGINAL
# AND *MUNDUS IMAGINALIS*

Throughout Jung's accounts of his imaginal experiences as recorded in the now published *Red Book* as well as his autobiography, and other publications, there is an exclusive focus on the "spontaneous encounter" with real fantasies i.e. fantasies that, like my "animals" gained a substantial "body", acted autonomously and had a feeling of having a quality of "immediacy" and a compelling presence. The generations of Jungian psychologists and beyond into the larger community of artists, poets, eco-psychologists and so on, have unquestioningly accepted Jung's account of his experiences as representing the true nature of the reality he was investigating ("the imaginal" to use Hillman's term for now).

"Jung's account" is the account given by that ego that is at first exterior to the images and thus could call them psychic facts, a description only possible to a consciousness that had thoroughly acquired the external positivistic form (the form of modern life). This ego then deliberately (i.e. with a programmatic intent) forces its way into becoming imaginal. The empirical ego becomes fictional, one image among others, as in a dream and then "discovers" a world of autonomous happenings, spontaneous events that have reality character, just as in dreams.

There is one decisive difference to this trance state when compared with ordinary dream states. The empirical ego does indeed become fictional but at the same time retains all the categories of experience that characterize the empirical ego. This becomes clear when we hear statements from Jung from within the trance state itself: [54]

*Then a most disagreeable thing happened. Salome . . . began to worship me. I said, "Why do you worship me?" She replied, "You are Christ." In spite of my objections she maintained this. I said, "This is madness," and became filled with sceptical resistance.* (96)

Here we can see that while Jung is engaging as one image to another as might happen in a dream, he also at the same time is *evaluating* or *interpreting* the image from the outside i.e. as an empirical ego would, while remaining *within* the imaginal state: "disagreeable" "madness", "sceptical resistance" are all evaluations that can be made only by an ego that has attained a form of consciousness we know as positivistic today, i.e. the modern ego.

This is only one example and I recommend Giegerich's masterful analysis of the *Red Book*, cited above for a conclusive analysis of this complex psychology at work.

Generations of people following Jung have naively accepted his ego's account of his "trance state" experiences thereby fostering an account of the reality that he proposed: an imaginal reality that has all the qualities of divine or enchanted Nature: immediate presence, numinosity, spontaneity, unintended, overwhelming, awe-inspiring and so on, just as nature appears to have been experienced in earlier times (shamanic period, hunters of the plain etc.).

In relation to this naive acceptance of the dream ego's interpretations of events, Giegerich writes: [55]

*Psychologically it is a grave mistake to privilege one element of a dream, fantasy, or psychic experience, for example the I, taking it literally by setting it up as a given existing outside the fantasy . . . and taking all other elements only as products of fantasy . . . . The I is just as internal to the fantasy as they are; it is an imaginal, "fantastic" I*

---

[54]   (Jung, 1989)

[55]   (Giegerich, 2010b)

*and needs to be seen through . . . . As psychologists we always have to take responsibility for the whole psychic phenomenon.* (372)

Giegerich is pointing to the folly of listening only to the dream ego's account of a dream as the truth of the dream—all the dream elements must be considered in arriving at truth. Yet as I have said, generations of followers have accepted Jung's accounts from his dream ego or "trance state ego" as the final word as to the reality and truth of his trance states.

This theoretical mistake has had significant repercussions on culture. Jung's ego descriptions of the nature of the imaginal reality that he wilfully entered have convinced countless others that there IS a way to return to sacred nature, there is a way to restore the divinity of animals (thereby saving the animal world and possibly ourselves, from extinction). We only have to do what Jung did, enter the inner world consciously through the practice of Active Imagination, or as modern artists strive to do, finding a rich harvest of images to express, manipulate and exploit.

At this point I want to stress that Giegerich is *not* saying that Jung has done anything wrong in so privileging the point of view of his ego nor in maintaining the categories of experience that properly belong to the empirical, positivistic form of consciousness while within the fictional or imaginal form of consciousness.

Ever the psychologist, Giegerich is saying first and foremost we should not, as psychologists follow blindly along with Jung—for us that would be a mistake, though it wasn't for Jung to do so. No, matters are more complicated than that: (ibid)

*. . . that Jung here took the I simply for granted "without questions asked" is not so much to be viewed as a failure of his, but rather a necessary ingredient of what the soul wanted to create with the whole process Jung underwent.* (372)

Here Giegerich is distinguishing between the dream ego's perspective and the intent of the soul in producing the dream in the first place. As psychologists we must privilege the *latter* if we want to arrive at the truth of the dream, trance etc.

When we do so take into account *all* the elements of the trance state that Jung and many modern artists, poets induce, then we do indeed arrive at a "more enhanced notion of the artists' trance state" that Hirsch seeks. It is however, very different from his and Corbin's and Hillman's notion of the *mundus imaginalis.* We must try to grasp this "enhanced notion" thoroughly if we are to comprehend any meaning that the "animal" soul has for us today. It is beyond the scope of this essay to fully develop the arguments that show that the unconscious psyche as conceived by Jung and indeed by the psychology of his time is a fabricated reality *not* a discovery of a natural object, or a recapitulation of spontaneous divine nature occurring now within the human being, in his psyche. The arguments are laid out convincingly in Sonu Shamdasani's scholarly work, *Jung and the Making of Psychology.* [56]

In this book he says:

*'Psychic Reality' is par excellence, the fabricated real. This is but to extend William James' remarks . . . that its (i.e. the psyche's) most remarkable 'property' was is capacity to present itself according to whatever theory one held about it.* (11)

Giegerich takes up this idea of the fabricated real more fully in his review of Shamdasani's book and in his own review of Jung's *Red Book.* (op.cit)

This review also bears careful reading in which he summarises just what the fabricated real is:

*The question emerges for us how and why the unconscious did come to be conceived as a natural object (thereby opening up the project of rescuing god or Meaning). The precondition was the great revolution from the metaphysical to the positivistic, scientistic stance at the beginning of the 19th century . . . the unconscious is the return . . . of the memory of and longing for metaphysics under the conditions of positivity.* (our modern form of consciousness—my insert) (209)

Shamdasani's publication of Jung's *Red Book* gives us amazing insight into the very formation of Jung's conception of the unconscious psyche. This would then be the definitive source

[56]   (Shamdasani, 2003)

that could settle for all time the question of the true nature of the psyche. Giegerich's analysis appeared soon after and establishes conclusively the nature of the psyche as the fabricated real.

A certain preparation however, is needed in order to know how to approach this article and indeed the *Red Book* in order to grasp Giegerich's arguments and finally his conclusion:

*Jung enters his fantasies with the categories of external reflection, namely with the distinction between fantasy and reality. Inside his fantasies, he views them from the outside and doubts the reality of their figures. It is as if a novel tried to pull the rug out from under its characters as only imagined, or as if we, while dreaming, turned around to the wild animal or to the murderous criminal chasing us and said to them, "you are only symbols.".*

*The fictions must not be innocently released into their fictional or fantasy character.* (402-403)

I think I can make clearer Giegerich's argument here and later, his conclusion about the true nature of the unconscious psyche that Jung *invented*, by this following comparison:

When Alice drops into Wonderland, she leaves the categories of thought that belong to empirical reality behind and becomes fictional herself, evaluating this new reality within its own terms (remember her long conversations with the caterpillar and Humpty Dumpty for example). While she is *inside* the fiction, i.e. is the fictional "I", each character opens up to its own interiority and depth, its own truth. In fact when she does at the end employ an *empirical* category of thought, "O, you all are just a pack of cards!" she moves out of fictional reality back into empirical reality where she becomes a little girl once more.

If we compare Alice's adventure with what we encounter when we enter the Internet reality of the Internet world of *Second Life* for example, this does not happen. We do "assume the facade of an avatar" but we never become that avatar i.e. we never become fictional like Alice did. Instead we enter still as the *empirical I*, carrying with us all our empirical categories of thought. We know and do not forget that the next avatar we meet on the street is a construction, like our own avatar, an "object", like empirical objects, only in the form of an image *positivized*. These images have no inner depth, or interiority. Any imaginal nature has been destroyed altogether. In other words we do not relate to a user's avatar in the way Alice relates to the imaginal figures of Wonderland. No one asks a Celtic warrior avatar about his initiation, his battles, his losses, his wisdom etc. Images are treated as empirical objects, related to by the empirical ego, *from within the fantasy*, with its empirical categories of thought.

As Giegerich says in the following passage (in regards the *Red Book*), the purpose of so regarding avatars and relating to other avatars, is not to falsify or undo the reality known as *Second Life*. *Their (i.e. the fictions) immediate sense of realness must be dissolved. The I is not allowed to simply swing itself onto Pegasus in order to let itself be carried wherever Pegasus wants* [as happened with Alice but which is disallowed in Second Life], *in the same way as the Red Book is not freely released into fantasy, as I showed above. This possibility has to be once and for all prevented in the Red Book by the intrusion into the fantasy itself of the critical reflection that the fictional figures are merely "symbols of" (this or that). The purpose of this operation, however, is by no means the undoing of the fantasy world. On the contrary . . .* [it is to set the fictionalizing] *up as absolutely real in a naturalistic or positivistic (already reflected) sense. Fantasy has to simulate the character of hard-core reality for its fictions . . . much like the new 20th. century technical medium of movies simulates reality so convincingly as to fool everyone.* (402-403)

Giegerich thus shows how Jung internalized the images of the natural or mental cosmos that formerly surrounded us, thereby fabricating an "inner" that simulates empirical reality. It was a long, extraordinarily painful process, to the point of torture and madness, as he reports in his *Leontocephalus* experience and throughout the *Red Book*. It involves a kind of turning inside out of reality, or rather a turning outside in. In this way Jung's life-long project of reclaiming Meaning in an age that keenly feels its loss was established.

Giegerich thus shows that this project is after all the soul's project, and that Jung was brought into participation with that project, to bring this fabricated reality into existence! In so doing, Jung was the augur-artist, "enacted the dream's hint", staying faithful to the soul all along. As he says in his letter to Read:

> *If the artist of today could only see what the psyche is spontaneously producing and what he, as a consciousness, is inventing, he would notice that the dream f.i. or the object is pronouncing (through his psyche) a reality from which he will never escape, because nobody will ever transcend the structure of the psyche.*

What is the soul's intent in so insisting (to the point of madness) on the installation of this *fabricated reality* that we commonly call the unconscious? We can get a hint of the meaning of this soul movement by noting this quote from Giegerich again: (quoted above)

> *The question merges for us how and why the unconscious did come to be conceived as a natural object (thereby opening up the project of rescuing god or Meaning). The precondition was the great revolution from the metaphysical to the positivistic, scientistic stance at the beginning of the 19th century . . . the unconscious is the return . . . of the memory of and longing for metaphysics under the conditions of positivity.*

The memory of and longing for metaphysics under the conditions of positivity! This is a difficult thought and I want to give some time to unpacking it with Giegerich's help as this analysis originates in his work.

First of all we must recognize that this longing is the *soul's own longing* to return to its former status of a metaphysical substance. Of course such longing implies that the soul has moved on to another *form* altogether. To accept the idea that the soul undergoes transformations in its reality status along with the corollary that history is therefore a record of such transformations (when viewed soulfully) is to accept and enter the psychology as a discipline of interiority—a discipline of the soul as established by Giegerich. [57]

---

[57]    (Giegerich, 2001)

Giegerich goes to great lengths to establish the current form of the soul throughout his works, but here I will refer to his latest book as a way into this question. [58]

In this book, *What is Soul?*, Giegerich begins with the fact that psychology today is generally conceived in a way that excludes soul altogether from consideration:

. . . *because it simply corresponded to the state of affairs, to the best insight possible . . . . In the history of the soul, not only the notion of God, but also that of its human counterpart, the notion of soul itself, had slowly dissolved into thin air. When in the second half of the 19th century Nietzsche proclaimed the death of God and Lange the demise of the soul, they did not merely present their personal and debateable views. They rather were, we might say, the mouthpiece of the objective psyche. They gave expression to what had in fact become of God and the soul respectively, in the course of the soul's historical opus.* (7-8)

He goes on to say:

*With the disappearance of the metaphysical concept and definition of the soul the soul itself did not also disappear. It entered a different logical status. It is a positivistic fallacy to think that the negation of the metaphysical soul led simply to nothing at all . . . .* (20)

The "dissolution into thin air" of the soul is a naturalistic picture of the soul's transformation into a reality status that no longer is *reflected* in any substantial form at all (natural object, thing, even image-as-object—all these are *metaphysical* in their logic). The soul today is occluded or hidden in the very form of consciousness that we *are* today. We can apprehend its movements only "within" that form of consciousness i.e. the realm of *living thought*. This is a very complex concept of soul that takes some getting used to but it *is* possible to get used to it and even to live soulfully within that living concept.

Why then has the soul gone to so much trouble to fabricate the reality we call the unconscious through the mouthpiece Jung, which later shows up in technology's simulated reality? The most

---

[58]   (Giegerich, 2012)

incisive argument I have found *for* this fabricated reality lies in Giegerich's brilliant analysis of neurosis, both individual neurosis and psychology's structural neurosis. [59] [60].

He shows that the "sick soul" both wants to hang on to the past (its metaphysical status) and go forward into the next stage (logical life, living thinking, beyond image). It does so by holding fast to the metaphysical under conditions of positivity. This complex soul condition shows up neurotically in human beings (who thus become *unwitting* mouthpieces of this soul movement) as for example a claustrophobic who inflates an ordinary positive fact (like an open field) with an absolute terror or panic although he or she is quite aware there is nothing actually threatening him or her. The positive fact becomes inflated with an Absolute principle that has broken through and which properly belongs to metaphysics but is not seen as such.

This "sick soul" phase is apparently what the soul needs to do in order to make the already achieved move to its new status *explicit* to itself. This need constitutes the archetypal background to the human need to not only act in the service of psychological development but also to make that act our truth by "saying it" into explicitness. So a young boy becomes a man, leaves home but must also be told by the community, "Now, you are a man!"

So too the soul "needs" to make explicit to itself that it has moved on from metaphysics to modernity (positive reality). The "cure" for neurosis simply is to align oneself to reality and face up to the losses that such an alignment incurs.

We can see from this analysis that Jung's project and his psychology, as initiated by the soul in its "sick soul" structure, is a neurotic one and for us in 2012, probably has only an historical interest, although at the time there was serious intent and a tremendous devotion to the project, under the impact of the soul's own need.

---

[59]    (Giegerich, 2012, p. 159ff)
[60]    (Giegerich, 2005b)

Since the soul has attained its new status of *logical life*, beyond image, we are now in a position to ask in a freshly informed manner, what are we to make of Jung's experience of *Leontocephalus* as well as the artistic "trance state" and as well, "everyman's" experience as represented by my own experience with animal images? What are we to now make of Lockhart's valuable observation as quoted above?

*I . . . was struck by what seems to be a gathering tide of apocalyptic dreams . . . I have observed the common elements of an extraordinary event in preparation, a sense of imminence, and . . . a simultaneous and increasing appearance of animals, animals coming, animals, watching, animals speaking, animals wanting to lead us, animals undergoing all manner of transformation?*

We could frame the question this way: In what way are these animal experiences that are occurring so impressively in picture form or sense-bound image during the trance-state that I discussed above, an unfoldment of the soul's logical life into modern cultural forms?

As we know, the soul is now working at a level of, in the form of, *Subject*. "The former soul as substance, as an "it", has completely gone under—died—into its own *concept* (soul had always been the implicit concept of Subject, or I, and personal identity)." [61] The soul no longer reflects itself in image which therefore has become ontologically reduced to mere shine, glitter, having no internal depth anymore, no longer opening up to spiritual meaning.

The reality status of soul today is that of the Subject, the I, logical *life*! Yet as I noted above "animal" images are appearing in an impressive "sensual embodied" form to Jung and today many others including myself. In order to fully understand this complex thought, let's take another look at the brilliant insight (quoted above) of Nietzsche that truly great mouthpiece of the soul:

---

[61]    (Giegerich, 2012, p. 289)

*Those instincts of wild, free, prowling man became turned backwards against man himself. Enmity, cruelty the delight in persecution, in surprises, change, destruction—the turning all these instincts against their own possessors: this is the origin of the "bad conscience." It was man, who, lacking external enemies and obstacles, and imprisoned as he was in the oppressive narrowness and monotony of custom, in his own impatience lacerated, persecuted, gnawed, frightened, and ill-treated himself; it was this animal in the hands of the tamer which beat itself against the bars of its cage; it was this being who, pining and yearning for that desert home of which it had been deprived, was compelled to create out of its own self, an adventure, a torture chamber, a hazardous and perilous desert—it was this fool this homesick and desperate prisoner—who invented the "bad conscience." But thereby he introduced that most grave and sinister illness, from which mankind has not yet recovered, the suffering of man from the disease called man, as the result of a violent breaking from his animal past, the result, as it were, of a spasmodic plunge into a new environment and new conditions of existence, the result of a declaration of war against the old instincts which up to that time had been the staple of his power, his joy, his formidableness.*

Viewing this quote as a document of the soul we can remove any prejudice that would suggest that we did something to ourselves (repressed our animal nature etc.) all those years ago and instead can regard this quote as the *speech of soul*, giving an account of its own "violent breaking from his animal past . . ." i.e. its own coming into being as soul life out of, but nonetheless remaining within biological life. We humans suffered this "violent break" and culture developed accordingly, much of which gave rise to the horrible practices that Nietzsche speaks along with the great advances that occurred.

We need to keep Giegerich's crucial concept of the psychological difference in mind when we think about the soul's movements through time (i.e. as history) *and* what we humans do, value, privilege etc. in response to those soul movements. For example the soul does seem to account for its own origins to itself in terms of a "violent break" with biological life, coming into being for example through the *logical* act of throwing the spear, or by confronting itself with death. [62] [63]

Once this rupture occurred *logically* i.e. in the Mind, we human beings were faced with *necessity*. Our existence as humans, i.e. as beings with minds was determined by the soul's coming into being this way. So, for example, until the soul had *established* itself as a more or less stable reality, we humans lived a form of existence known anthropologically as the hunter-gather period which lasted hundreds of thousands of years. We were compelled to *ritually* re-enact the coming-into-being of the soul (hunting, spearing, as ritualized) because those empirical acts were at that time also *logical* acts that brought the soul into existence, for as long as the ritual lasted. It had to be repeated until stabilized.

We were also *free* to do things to one another (as Nietzsche proposes) that did not invoke soul at all but were merely acting out of desire to hurt others, persecute, etc, all acts being made possible by the development of a consciousness "outside" of nature but remaining in the all-too-human realm of personal satisfaction, revenge etc. In this way our human subjective consciousness deviates from the soul's movements by clinging to forms that have outlived their soul purpose. We can lag behind as it were. Giegerich has shown how today, for example, our subjective consciousness has remained "stuck" in metaphysics while the soul has advanced to its present logical status beyond substantial forms altogether, creating a dissociated structure in modern consciousness. [64]

Related to this human "lagging behind" the movements of soul, Giegerich also further demonstrates what happens psychically when subjective consciousness is presented with a new soul truth and refuses what it knows to be true, preferring to hang on to past truths that no longer reflect reality. This demonstration can

---

[62]   (Giegerich, 2008, p. 202ff)
[63]   (Giegerich, 2012, p. 51)
[64]   (Giegerich, 2010c, p. 261)

be very clearly seen in his examination of Jung's well known early experience as reported in *Memories Dreams, Reflections* which includes his vision of God shitting on the cathedral. [65] Giegerich shows that Jung at first was engaged fully in a thought process, the event of a thought, a thinking that was occurring through him and by him as he thought it. So far then Jung's subjective consciousness had risen up to the modern status of soul i.e. in its current form as *subject*, an I, *logical life* only, beyond imagistic or picture-thinking.

However, instead of thinking the thought through to the end, to its utmost conclusion, Jung refused the thought, refused the soul's pressing into him in order to come into existence through him. He resisted bringing his subjective consciousness into alignment with the current reality status of soul which, in Jung, was "speaking" the end of its reflecting itself in any substantial form and therefore was also speaking the demise of Jung's and our embeddedness in nature. What happens next is of great relevance to my proposal regarding the meaning of animal images presenting themselves to us in trance-states etc.

Jung's refusal of the second half of the thought he was having resulted in its having to appear to him, not in the form of *living thinking* as was intended, but as "forced back down and held down on the semantic level . . . as a *new separate event* in the story" i.e. as an image, positivized coming towards Jung's observing ego, no longer able to recognize the initial thought that "wanted to" think itself fully through him as his thought, as *thinking*! [66] [67]

Now we are close to a possible meaning of the "animal" soul appearing as "sense-bound" images i.e. images appearing under conditions of positivity. It seems clear to me from the foregoing discussion that they do not mean a resurgence of the 12th century *mundus imaginalis*! Consciousness has transformed well beyond that stage where image still was transparent to Meaning, truth

---

[65]   (Jung, 1965)

[66]   (Giegerich, 2007a, pp. 11-52)

[67]   (Giegerich, 2012, pp. 108-120)

and infinite depths with itself. Rather, the proliferation of animal dreams, or animal presences interpenetrating with subjective consciousness, as in my case or Jung's *Leontocephalus* occurring today are all indicative of an aspect of the soul's logical life that wants to think itself out through the augur-artist, or *to come into existence* through the augur-artist's enactment but *at the level of logical life* which is the current status of soul today —the *Subject*!

This *animal* aspect of the soul's logical life is, however, as in Jung's case, being held down in positivized image form, thus appearing to us "spontaneously", "autonomously" with "immediacy" and "numinosity", in its *otherness* (but no longer a self-other relation) because of our deep *human* heritage of privileging the denial of the body or our animal origins, holding them in contempt, despising matter, as Jung writes elsewhere (see quote in Introduction).

So, when the soul wishes to *think* that aspect of its own life (the "animal", the "sensual", the "wild" etc.) into existence through us, we refuse it, based on our prejudice towards the same over millennia of civilization, as Nietzsche tells us.

We can now look freshly at one aspect of my own case, i.e. with my *interpenetration of images*, i.e. when I experience the animal presence interpenetrating with my humanness, with its full animal power and grace. First of all I can affirm that my own life certainly included the "inheritance" of despising my animal origins. This contempt did not occur on the personal empirical level. I was, in my subjective consciousness, as free as any other flower-child of the sixties and seventies. No, this fear and contempt showed up in my sustained and determined refusal to "enter the wild" in thought. I held to what I knew with a grip of iron, utterly defeating others who wanted to introduce me to something unknown, unfamiliar, even an insight into myself. They were rejected out of hand. While I was in my undergraduate years I studied the dictionary, one word a day. Was it to increase my ability to make distinctions, enrich my vocabulary? Not bit of it! I studied hard that way so as not to be "caught with my pants down" which is an interesting image to come right now.

I did not want to be caught "not knowing" so I stayed locked in my "little suburban mind". I even dreamed of a monstrous whale leaking sperm copiously, lying cramped in a little suburban pool—a rather interesting picture of the psychological difference, it occurs to me now.

So the refusal operates at a level where it can interfere with the soul's intention. It is a *logical* refusal, a way of thinking that "observes" the other as inferior and holds it down that way. But because the soul is determinative, as Giegerich shows us it WILL have its way and so I began to have these "impressive" animal appearances, as Jung had his scandalous cathedral image as a boy and his *Leontocephalus* experience as a mature man.

Giegerich's analysis of the soul phenomenology of these self-induced trance experiences shows that whatever these "animal" experiences mean they cannot mean a return to the *mundus imaginalis*, as thought by Corbin or Hirsch nor to an imaginal "in between" world as thought by Hillman—all these conceptions being modern reconstructions of 12ᵗʰ century mystical "picture thinking" in which body becomes spirit and spirit becomes body (whatever body and spirit meant in those days). They instead mean that a very complex modern psychology is at work deep with the psyche of modern human beings, Jung being the exemplar of this complexity—a psychology that includes:

a centuries-long sustained human habit of logical contempt towards our material and biological (animal) being; a human "lagging behind" the historical movements of soul in its self-transformations, including its "animal" aspect; the soul's reaching a status of reality that is beyond image, beyond substance, beyond the previous metaphysical status of reality; the soul's self-presentation as "sick soul" expressed as cleaving to its old status as metaphysical "substance" while at the same time, advancing to its present form of logical life, this "sickness" resulting in metaphysical truths presenting themselves under modern conditions of positivity;

Jung's remaining faithful to this "sick soul" stage and fabricating a reality that he called the unconscious, Hillman developing it into the imaginal, Corbin interpreting the *mundus imaginalis*, which Hirsch endorses as the more "enhanced notion" of his "artistic trance states".

All these modern conceptions create a real appearance of the "animal" soul in a way that satisfies longings for a reconnection with our (imagined) oneness with nature, biological life, that once *"had been the staple of his power, his joy, his formidableness"*. In fact they represent a kind of neurotic structure—a half-way house so that the soul can make its transformation to pure logical life explicit to itself (by pushing off its formerly held metaphysical status with the simple declaration of its current untruth.) This neurotic structure *must* present to the dreaming or entranced ego a real appearance of "animal presences" in full "sensual, embodied form" so that the ego (as that aspect of soul that is external to itself) is convinced that its former "glory" as metaphysical reality still obtains as truth while simultaneously seeing through it as an untruth (Jung's conception of *psychic* facts, the *as if* kind of reality etc.)

Once this neurotic structure is seen through, the entire structure can reach its conclusion and consciousness can come home to its present form as logical life, the *Subject*.

So far then I have explored the kinds of experiences that lead many to conclude that "animal" soul today could mean something like a reconnection with sacred nature, or of the divinity of the animal, as we apparently once experienced along with the Meaning that such a connection bestowed on our lives. It turns out that such longings are only that—longings for what is no longer possible. Instead we can see that a complex psychology is at work behind such appearances, one that is thoroughly modern in character and belongs to our time only. We can see that the soul IS presenting such experiences with animal images but really has something in mind quite different from what it was in the past concerned with.

Now after this long discussion with its many threads, we perhaps can see what "animal" soul simply cannot mean. We can therefore now turn to what it *could* mean, in terms of the modern reality status of the soul (logical *life*).

What follows now is my tentative thesis concerning the "animal" soul:

*The interpenetration of "animal" image with the dream or trance "I" is an imagistic presentation of what can only complete itself at the level of mind! The soul is trying to think out through the human, the nature of itself as* living *thinking which includes the animal aspect of thinking!*

# THE "ANIMAL" AS AN ASPECT OF THE SUBJECT

We can only grasp this thesis in thought. Any other approach (imagistic, positivistic) simply holds down the soul's intention to past forms (e.g. metaphysical substances). I think I can bring this mystery of the soul into reach though by sharing something more of my own efforts and experience towards reaching this thesis that I am proposing.

Let's start with images and, by viewing them with soul, allow them to sublate, distil into living thinking, as which the soul "exists" today (i.e. when soul presents through the modern human being). Let's begin with my historic clinging to knowledge, refusing to go under at any cost as I shared earlier.

I began to shift from my "stuckness" with the following dream. I call it a dream of humility:

*I am in a room with Chuck Norris. He decides to meet me in combat after a playful spar in which I block one or two strikes. I now need to prepare for the fight. As I do so, we are moving towards a secret monastery outside town. I wonder increasingly what it is I think I am doing. There is no way in the world I can fight Norris. People are gathering in the auditorium. I try to practice by doing basic katas from my own training years ago—woefully inadequate. Who am I kidding? They will see through me completely. What a sham! This is a mockery! I move towards a young boy.*

*Now I am in a room. My bravado is useless. Any thought of I know what to do next slips away fast. In this room where I am in the centre and others line the walls, watching. A young man comes up to me and shows me a book—a box red with a red string running through it. This is his solution to the problem of cause and effect. "How long do you think I have been working on this problem?" he says, faintly mocking, adding, "a good deal longer than you!" I do not have the faintest idea of what he is showing me. I feel humiliated, knowing nothing or near to it.*

*The room erupts in chanting. More people go around the room, taking turns to chat about this or that existential problem. One man looking at me has tears of compassion for my plight.*

*I am being submitted to a barrage of knowledge that I know nothing about. It is an ordeal. I do not know what to do next and I begin to weep. All my own ideas, plans, purpose, were washed away in my ordeal. The master is in the room too. I am left with no words. He gets up and moves away and I simply follow him. We enter ordinary reality, a house. He sits down and I come in. He says gently that I must not sit down, as we put on sandals. We are going to meet a great man who lives in ordinary life.*

This dream began to *initiate* me. I began to surrender. The locus of knowledge had now shifted away from me as ego to the *other* within, as the dream says. I began to feel that I did not *possess* knowledge as much as experienced it "coming towards me". This shift away from the ego as centre began to show up in the style of my artistic work—my writing. I found that if I *led* with knowing i.e. writing down what I already *knew*, or leading with my thinking function, then my writing dried up, and I revealed myself to be rather a poor thinker indeed. However if I began with what emerged into consciousness, with what *quickened* within me and followed *its* hints, then a very different kind of writing emerged. It lacked formal precision, or predictable prosaic structures, but it was *alive*!

At first this style was very disconcerting as it took me way beyond the established and recognized forms of prose that would receive acceptance in journals etc. It insisted on itself during the entire duration of my Ph.D. program, which was cause for tremendous anxiety. I could not write any other way and yet what would Academia think of it? I still look back on those years of toil and wonder if any other Ph.D. has been born from a literal dream. Yes, my entire program began with a dream and by my methodology of following the hint of the dream no matter what. What began with a trickle soon became a torrent. I wrote 10-12 hours a day for three years. I had to "invent" a methodology that would support such work and finally, it was accepted. A record of my process through those years can be found in my book, *Living in Uncertainty, Living with Spirit*, an early attempt to begin to comprehend what I had done. [68]

As this process deepened over the years, I began more to trust this style of writing that I had been engaged in for many years. It was and still remains a style that I describe elsewhere as:

. . . *a spontaneous weaving of realities that we normally keep well apart. The writing moves from a memory to a dream to a reflection of an external event, to an etymological study of a word, to the words of another author until the usual separation of inner and outer dissolves. The process involves memories of a kind of dual consciousness, interweaving of past present and future, inner and outer reality, along with philosophical thoughts expressed in direct speech which come to the author quite spontaneously.*

This description comes close to Lockhart's augury in which he asks what would happen to literature if we wrote according to Jung's famous dictum: everything belongs! [69]

*For me Jung's secret is that "everything belongs," and for this reason, I get very curious about what is excluded, abandoned, pushed out of view, out of sight. In the dictionary, it is never the meanings that are pushed aside. They always belong. Every dictionary has them. Has them with numbers. Has them in the main text. But there is "something else" sometimes, but always set off from the text, set off in parentheses. I'm referring, of course, to the etymology of the word. In parentheses, set off, as the dictionary itself says of the practice, set off as a digression, an interruption of continuity, an*

---

[68]   (Woodcock, 2007)
[69]   (Lockhart, 1987)

*interval, an interlude, something independent and unnecessary to
the surrounding text . . . .*

*But if we get into the parentheses, inside those digressions, into
those interruptions of continuity, those interludes, something else
begins to happen. And just at this point a thought intrudes itself
which should of course be in a parenthesis but I can't do it. I think
just now of Jacques Derrida and his "deconstruction" approach,
which in connection with these parentheses would have us turn
them around facing the other way ) ( so that the main text is
captured by these little enclosures and the digressions, the interludes,
the interruptions are set free. But then you would ask: how could
we have any rational discourse if we start breaking the rules that
are so basic? Well is that the point? To have rational discourse? Or,
might it not be to show what is there in one's experience, all of it,
uncensored by parentheses? In fact, didn't depth psychology begin in
an attempt to abolish parentheses—nothing excluded, everything
belongs? I know that the simplest way to overcome writer's block is
to forget parentheses all punctuation in fact as poetry has discovered
and let everything have its say everything on equal footing the silly
idea mingling with the most profound I once had a dream that I
would have to write a paper on the importance of being silly—but
I'm aware now that it's time to get back to order, to return the
punctuation, to bring the parentheses back, to find the trail of
rational discourse once again. I was getting close to breaking out
with . . . but I "parentheseized" it! (105)*

Breaking out! Yes, into the wilderness of thought where the
wild animals roam! As I read his passage, increasingly there was
a "feeling" within that thought of horses breaking out of a corral
and breaking into stride, free on the plain at last.

In writing *this* book, I practised my art. I did not start off with
an agenda, a point I wanted to make and then making it. I had
no idea I would end up here at all. I followed my "nose". I went
down trails that opened up suddenly in the brush. Some trails
dried up and I was "lost" again in the wild. Books spilled over
my desk onto the floor as my blood quickened. I remembered
a quote from years ago. The reference leaped out at me from

the shelf, eager to be included. Two books, both from Lockhart crashed loudly, unexpectedly, onto my keyboard. What do you want, Russ? Now, his quote lies just above this paragraph. Ok, Ok I get it! You're in!

I cringed with fear, heated up with passion, trembled with excitement, ached with tiredness.

Yet, with all this "spontaneity" I can equally claim that this book had been arranged all along. I simply made the outcome i.e. my thesis concerning the "animal" soul explicit to myself.

All those books that now lie on desk, floor, and table are not randomly chosen books. I chose them as one being pulled towards the unknown future, and, as an augur-artist I followed the hint, not knowing where it would lead but knowing with a certainty that it was leading somewhere, somewhere that I already "knew". Now, I *know*! It was there all the time and I simply had to put in the work of making the thought explicit. My wife often reminds me, "John, you have been saying that for years!" It has taken many years, since my first encounters with the dream animals to make this thought explicit.

The "animal" as an aspect of soul life in its present status as subject, as absolute interiority, can only be discerned *within the syntax* of the artistic production. In my case this means my writing, even in writing this book.

If my thesis is right then you, dear reader may be able to discern, with the "eyes" of the soul, some of the animal movements occurring at the level of *living thinking*, "within" my thoughts that lie here on these pages. Within the content of my book i.e. the "animal" soul, if I am on the right path here, we also may, with the mind only, detect an animal presence *stirring within* the writing style itself.

What do you "sense"?

# ADDENDUM

What would happen if the Coming Guest actually appeared?
Well, listen to this true story . . .

C. G. Jung wrote to Sir Herbert Read in 1960, one year
before Jung died. He is addressing the future and our role in
bringing the future into actuality:

*The great problem of our time is that we don't understand what
is happening to the world. We are confronted with the darkness of
our soul, the unconscious. It sends up its dark and unrecognizable
urges. It hollows out and hacks up the shapes of our culture and
its historical dominants. who is the awe-inspiring guest who knocks
at our door portentously? Fear precedes him, showing that ultimate
values already flow towards him . . . we have simply got to listen to
what the psyche spontaneously says to us . . . . It is the great dream
which has always spoken through the artist as mouthpiece. All his
love and passion (his "values") flow towards the coming guest.*

I was seeing a client last week who worked in IT and earns a
lot of money. He also drinks himself into oblivion on a regular
basis, culminating in a violent attack on his wife, hence therapy.
When we touched on the subject of the future he told me he was
anxious about money and the future was a black hole for him,
obviously an image of sheer terror!

When *love* flows towards the unknown future as Jung describes
the image is not of terror but one of a "coming guest", an image
that evokes the possibility of a hospitable welcome. When fear or
even terror (my client and others) flows towards the future, then
'black holes' "catastrophes", in short, apocalyptic imagery is called
forth, evoking more terror, more resistance, more pathology,

more cultural forms (Security, Insurance, foreign policy based on worse case scenarios, etc.) that only succeed in bringing these fears into actuality.

The future becomes what we fear most!

*Can* we instead turn to the unknown future with love, greeting the awesome guest with hospitality and love? Is it *possible* for us to do this?

Let me take you back to 1906, to the Sydney art gallery where an exhibition of pre-Raphaelite paintings is being shown. The central piece on exhibit is a picture by Holman Hunt entitled: *The Light of the World.*

First take a look at the picture in the context of our discussion about the Coming Guest:

Figure 4

So here is an image of the awe inspiring guest knocking portentously on our door. This is what everyone in Sydney is waiting for, with longing anticipation. So what happens when he turns up? The following report is drawn from the Daily Telegraph, 1906:

*Before 2 o'clock yesterday afternoon, almost 2000 people were waiting for the doors of the art gallery to open, and before the doors were closed again at 5 0'clock, 23080 people had passed through the turnstiles to see Holman Hunt's picture, "The Light of the World." The crowd was enormous. Once or twice, when the doors were closed against any further invasion of the building until those inside passed out, thousands gathered in solid mass against the entrance door and waited for admittance. Then when the doors were opened there was an extraordinary struggle. Women had their hats broken, blouses deranged, blouse belts and sashes torn or broken. Men pushed forward from the back, and men pushed backward from the front. Out of the struggling came the crying of terrified children Here two mites sobbed a request to be put through a window so they might speed home from a hitherto unknown battle of humans; there two policemen carried to a corner the stiffened figure of a woman who had fainted. Clearing themselves from the contortions of the crowd, many women found out spaces, where they touched up the little damages that had befallen them—hats were straightened out, tousled hair made tidy, and dresses smoothed down—for all the world like an indignant number of hens preening feathers after unexpectedly half-drowned with a deluge of water.*

*Then came the closing of the doors again, with the police perspiring like firemen in a stokehold in their efforts to cut off the crown that was pouring in. Dozens of younger men clambered up and jumped through open windows. It was a maddened race of modern pilgrims to a new shrine—a riot of curiosity.*

*Up stairs to the big picture the crowd went in endless clattering procession—old men, young men, boys, women of all ages, and little children holding each other's hands. In front of "the Light of the World" they stood and wondered if they had found what they had expected—wondered if they were pleased or disappointed. It was impossible to gauge the thoughts of the crowd—to understand what the picture said to the thousands of eyes that flung eagerly upwards to discover its possessions for their keeping, its rewards for their curiosity, its lessons for their remembrance.*

*Always the faces remained unchanged. One felt that the wave that had rushed itself through the doorways and gallery should here have had its climax of enthusiasm at the foot of the picture, but it was not there. Almost within a yard of the great work a girl busied herself in re-arranging a feather in her companion's hat; and two little lads, bent half over the railing by the weight of the crowd, discussed vehemently business connected with the sale and purchase of a pair of pigeons. In a dozen different places in the crowd, one heard the men who talked of the aims of art; the man who praises or blames the technique of the picture; and the girl who described the picture as "Nice!"*

*A few minutes in front of the picture sufficed most of those who came, and then they wandered around the galleries. Never before did art receive so much attention in Sydney.*

Now in 2011, one hundred years on, what can we make of this extraordinary event? Clearly the Sydney art lovers *were* turning to the *Coming Guest* with anticipation, love, longing, and enthusiasm, at first anyway! Then it all went wrong! As we saw, the longing was quickly quenched at the moment that one might expect fulfilment. The reason for this I propose is that, for the people of Sydney in 1906, as it is for us now even more, the outer positive reality of the painting occludes, rather than opens up to the soul factor that animates the picture. While the *intimation* of the coming guest opened hearts, quelled noisy minds, and deepened anticipation and welcome, the positive fact of the coming guest's arrival i.e. as a painting that was only experienced in its positivity in accord with our historical times completely quelled all anticipations and restored instead the empirical ego to its ascendant position in consciousness.

We need not bemoan our stupidity nor do we need to smilingly patronize those 1906 citizens who after all are also us. The fact that the soul is now fundamentally occluded (hidden, closed off) within what has therefore become "positive reality" (the world that we ordinarily feel to be bereft of meaning today, leading to widespread anxiety etc.) is the soul's own doing and gives us the opportunity to be initiated into the reality of the soul *as such*, i.e. as *interiority*, unencumbered by its historical states of reflection in any form of outer reality.

Perhaps *absolute interiority* is the coming guest!

# REFERENCES

Adler, G., & Jaffe, A. (Eds.). (1975). *C. G. Jung Letters* (Vols. 2 (1951-1961)). (R. F. Hull, Trans.) London: Routledge & Kegan Paul, Ltd.

AE. (1965). *The Candle of Vision*. New York: University Books.

Barfield, O. (1977). *The Rediscovery of Meaning and other essays*. San Rafael: The Barfield Press.

Campbell, J. (1984). *Primitive Mythology*. New York: Penguin.

*Film Movement*. (2011, April 18). Retrieved from Film Movement: http://www.filmmovement.com

Giegerich, W. (2001). *The Soul's Logical Life*. Frankfurt: Peter Lang.

_____(2003, December 2). *The End of Meaning and the Birth of Man*. Retrieved December 13, 2010, from http://www.cgjungpage.org/index.php?option=content&task=view&id=332

_____(2004a). After Shamdasani. *Spring 71*, 193-213.

_____(2004b). Response to the Responses by Mogenson, Miller, Beebe, and Pulver. *Journal of Jungian Theory and Practice, 6*(1), 107-124.

_____(2005b). *Collected English Papers: Volume 1: The Neurosis of Psychology.* New Orleans: Spring Journal, Inc.

_____(2006). Closure and Setting Free or the Bottled Spirit of Alchemy and Psychology. *Spring 74 Alchemy,* 31-62.

_____(2007a). Psychology as Anti-Philosophy: C. G. Jung. *Spring 77,* 11-53.

_____(2007b). *Technology and the Soul.* New Orleans: Spring Journal Books.

_____(2008). *Collected English Papers Volume III: Soul Violence.* New Orleans: Spring Journal Inc.

_____(2010a). God Must Not Die! C.G. Jung's Thesis of the One-Sidedness of Christianity. *Spring 84,* 11-71.

_____(2010b). Liber Novis, that is, The New Bible, A First Analysis of C. G. Jung's Red Book. *Spring 83,* 361-413.

_____(2010c). *The Soul Always Thinks.* New Orleans: Spring.

_____(2012). *What is Soul?* New Orleans: Spring Journal Books.

_____, Miller, D. L., & Mogenson, G. (2005a). *Dialectics and Analytical Psychology: The El Capitan Canyon Seminar.* New Orleans: Spring Journal, Inc.

Hillman, J. (1989). Cosmology for Soul, From Universe to Cosmos. *Sphinx,* 2, 17-33.

_____(2008). *Animal Presences.* Putnam: Spring Publications, Inc.

Hirsch, E. (2002). *The Demon and the Angel: Searching for the Source of Artistic Inspiration.* Orlando: Harcourt Books.

Jung, C. G. (1965). *Memories, Dreams, Reflections.* New York: Vintage Books.

_____(1988). *Nietzsche's Zarathustra: Notes of the Seminar given in 1934-1939.* (J. L. Jarrett, Ed.) Princeton: Princeton University Press.

_____(1989). *Analytical Psychology: Notes on the seminar given in 1925.* (W. McGuire, Ed.) Princeton: Princeton University Press.

_____(2009). *The Red Book.* (S. Shamdasani, Ed., S. Shamdasani, M. Kyburz, & J. Peck, Trans.) New York: W.W. and Norton & Company.

Lockhart, R. A. (1987). *Psyche Speaks: A Jungian Approach to Self and World.* Wilmette: Chiron.

Rilke, R. M. (2011). *Rainer Maria Rilke > quotes.* Retrieved April 20, 2011, from GoodReads: http://www.goodreads.com/author/quotes/7906.Rainer_Maria_Rilke

Rodriguez, A. (1993). *Book of the Heart: The Poetics, Letters, and Life of John Keats.* Hudson: Lindisfarne Press.

Shamdasani, S. (2003). *Jung and the Making of Modern Psychology.* Cambridge: Cambridge University Press.

Tacey, D. (2010). Ecopsychology and the Sacred: The Psychological Basis of the Environmental Crisis. *Spring 83*, 329-353.

Tarnas, R. (1991). *The Passion of the Western Mind: Understanding the Ideas That Have Shaped Our World.* Reading: Cox and Wyman Ltd.

Woodcock, J. C. (2007). *Living in Uncertainty Living with Spirit.* Lincoln: iUniverse.

_____(2011). *The Imperative.* Bloomington: iUniverse, Inc.

_____(2011, July). *Weaving Voices.* Retrieved August 11, 2011, from www.lighthousedownunder.com.

John C. Woodcock holds a doctorate in Consciousness Studies (1999). His thesis articulates the process and outcome of a spiritual ordeal that lasted twenty years. At first it seemed to John that he was undergoing a purely personal psychological crisis but over time, with assistance from his various mentors, he discovered that he was also participating in the historical process of a transformation of the soul as reflected in the enormous changes occurring in our culture, often referred to as apocalyptic.

As these powerful and determinative processes took hold of John's being, his task was at first simply to contain them while somehow carrying on with ordinary life. John's first books, *Living in Uncertainty Living with Spirit*, *Making of a Man: Initiation Through the Divine Mother*, and *Transformation of the World* describe how he managed to live in a dual reality, since for many years he could not reconcile his inner experience of soul life and external ordinary life.

Over time John began to comprehend how external reality, seemingly so bereft of soul, is indeed itself a manifestation of soul. Soul and world were found to be a unity of differences. This discovery opened up the possibility of discerning soul movement from within present external reality, comprising hints of the unknown future. John's next three books, *The Coming Guest, The Imperative,* and *Hearing Voices,* explore this idea more fully by describing the initiatory process and outcome of a human being's becoming a vehicle for the expression of the unknown future, through the medium of his or her art.

John's latest book, *Animal Soul* establishes a firm theoretical ground for the claim that the soul is urging us towards the development of new inner capacities that he calls the augur-artist mind—the mind that can discern and artistically render the hints of the unknown future.

John currently lives in Sydney with his wife Anita where he teaches, writes, and consults with others concerning their soul life. He is also a practicing Jungian therapist.